CONTENTS

PREFACE

The Sydney district is one of the great wildflower regions of the world. Over 1500 species occur within an hour's drive of the city centre. It is not uncommon for suburban bushland patches to have 300 to 500 species, and for larger national parks to protect up to 1000 species. The sandstone heaths and woodlands of Ku-ring-gai Chase National Park, Muogamarra Nature Reserve, Royal National Park and elsewhere are renowned for their floral displays in spring which rival those of other famous wildflower zones, such as the Grampians (Vic), the Kalbarri sand plains (WA) and the Wallum coastline (Qld).

With such a large flora, it was not possible to include all the species in a book of this size. Selection of the 268 plants was based on a number of criteria. Most of the wildflowers illustrated selected themselves — they are the colourful and common plants, conspicuous because of the nature of their growth habit or their flowers, and which force themselves onto the attention of the passer-by. Some species, less widespread, but interesting and conspicuous within their restricted range, have also been selected. A conscious effort was made to balance the great variety of species from sandstone areas with wildflowers from the shale-clay areas of western Sydney.

Most of the plants illustrated are, of course, not exclusively Sydney species. Only 34 are restricted in their distribution to the Sydney region, but the rest extend into the adjacent Blue Mountains, Southern Highlands and to sandstone areas north of Broken Bay. Some are found throughout the State and indeed in other States. Of those illustrated, 122 also occur in Victoria and 153 in Queensland.

This book aims to encourage an appreciation of Sydney's floral beauty and variety, and to foster the conservation and wise management of plant communities so they will be here for future generations to enjoy. There are wildflower communities just around the corner or just a short drive away for everyone living in or visiting the city of Sydney.

INTRODUCTION

'The great quantity of New Plants Mr Banks and Dr Solander collected in this place occasioned my giving it the name of Botany Bay.'

Journal of Captain James Cook, 6th May 1770

From the first days of European discovery, the wonderful variety and uniqueness of the flora impressed visitors to the Sydney region. For the botanist Joseph Banks and his assistant Daniel Solander on board Cook's *Endeavour*, the eight day stay at Botany Bay was like a visit to a new world where everything was a fresh discovery. In these few days, Banks collected over 80 new species and filled over 2400 sheets of drying paper with his collection. Many of the species taken back to England, including *Banksia serrata*, *Hibbertia scandens*, *Kennedia rubicunda* and *Westringia fruticosa*, can still be found in the sandy woodlands and coastal heaths in the vicinity of modern-day Kurnell.

The Banks' collection aroused enormous scientific interest in England and Europe, so much so that the great Swedish botanist Carl Linnaeus even suggested that the newly discovered Great Southern Land should be named 'Banksia'. This wasn't to be, but in an appropriate tribute, Linnaeus' son named that quintessentially Australian genus *Banksia* in recognition of Banks' discoveries.

Scientific interest in this mysterious new botanical world heightened after the establishment of a permanent settlement in Port Jackson in 1788 and as the surrounding countryside was explored. Collections of living and dried plants and seeds were sent to England by people like John White, the First Fleet Surgeon General, and his assistant Denis Considen. By 1794 seed collected from Australian wattle was being cultivated in England. Banks, now chief scientific officer at the Royal Botanic Gardens at Kew, employed George Caley in 1800 and Robert Brown in 1802 to collect for him and their travels included trips to western Sydney, Nepean, The Oaks and the northern beaches. This early exploration was followed by the contribution of botanists like Allan Cunningham and F.W. Sieber who, in the 1820s, collected further afield, including the Illawarra and Blue Mountains.

Gradually, in the nineteenth century, the wealth of Sydney's flora became known to science, described and named. But at the same time, European settlement was bringing change and destruction of natural habitats. The first farms were on the better soils derived from Wianamatta Shales around Parramatta, Windsor and Camden, and on the fertile river flats of the Hawkesbury and Nepean. Tall forests of Sydney Blue Gum, Blackbutt and Turpentine in Lane Cove Valley and elsewhere were exploited for valuable timbers used in housing, fences, wharf piles and the other requirements of an expanding population. By 1900, little remained of the extensive Ironbark–Turpentine forests of the inner west as settlement radiated from Sydney Cove.

Land regarded as unfit for farming, too shrubby, infertile, steep or difficult of access, was bypassed and generally left uncleared. Fortunately for Sydney, these are the very areas where our flora is at its most diverse. Many of these sandstone areas became national parks or, as around Sydney Harbour, protected by military reserves. On the clay and shale of western Sydney, only remnants of the original bush remain, although some of the better patches, like Castlereagh, Windsor Park, Bents Basin, Mitchell Park and Scheyville, have been recently given protection as reserves under National Parks and Wildlife Service legislation. These contain important fragments of the plant communities which once covered the entire Cumberland Plain.

Boundaries of the Sydney region

For the purpose of this book, the Sydney region is that area bounded in the north by Broken Bay, in the north-west by the Hawkesbury River, to the west by the Nepean River and in the south by a line drawn from Maddens Plains through Appin to The Oaks in the south-west. From Sydney City by road, these boundaries are approximately 50 km to the north, 50 km to the south, 55 km to the west and 75 km to both the north-west and south-west extremities at Wisemans Ferry and The Oaks respectively. Much of the central part of this area is heavily urbanised and the western Cumberland Plain, largely cleared for farming and grazing in the early years of settlement, is now subject to increasing pressures from housing subdivision and suburban growth. Despite this, bushland patches remain where wildflowers can be found. However, the focal points of most wildflower devotees are the national parks on sandstone areas north and south of Sydney, for it is there that the most colourful displays and the greatest variety occur.

The nature of the environment

The distribution of specific plant species is influenced by a number of factors. The nature of the soil, aspect, drainage, shelter, height above sea level, temperature and rainfall patterns all help determine which plants grow in a certain location. The major role of underlying rock types in distribution patterns is clearly seen in the Sydney region. In general, plants can be divided into those that grow in sandy soils derived from Hawkesbury Sandstone and those that prefer the richer shale and clay soils derived either from the Wianamatta Group or the Narrabeen Group. Within this basic division, there are many variations, such as sandstone enriched with eroded shale soils, sandstone with laterite capping, deep sands and alluvium of more recent age, shale–sandstone interface, wet sandy zones and a few high fertility areas produced by eroded volcanic necks and dolerites. The subtle influence of soil on plant distribution is what makes walking through the bush and the identification of native plants such an interesting experience.

Sydney City is built on a base of Hawkesbury Sandstone. Sydney Harbour lies in a dissected valley carved by ancient rivers through the sandstone. Sandstone outcrops form a wide wedge north to Broken Bay and Brisbane Water and north-west to Wisemans Ferry and Dharug NP. It gradually rises like the side of a bowl to about 240 metres at Maroota and West Head. The raised plateau is cut by V-shaped valleys between a maze of narrow ridges. Along the coast, the sandstone has broken off to form impressive sheer cliffs. South of Sydney, the Nepean Ramp forms the other rim of the sandstone bowl, extending south beyond the Georges River and Royal NP. The Water Board land and Military Reserve between Campbelltown and the coast are almost all sandstone based. The Nepean Ramp gradually rises to 380 metres near O'Hares Creek before linking up with the 670 metres Robertson Plateau beyond Wollongong.

Soil derived from Hawkesbury Sandstone is poor in mineral plant food and is often quite shallow. However, it does contain particles of weathered mud and clay and is enriched by decaying plant matter. Bushfires add ash and valuable minerals to the sand, but also reduce plant cover and increase evaporation rates. Away from the plateau, the slopes and valleys have deeper soils enriched by the humus which is washed down the slopes. The hillsides can support taller trees and thicker shrub cover, especially if they are south facing and protected for some of the day from the sun and drying winds. The damper and shadier gullies often contain tall straight trees and large understorey shrubs, with elements of rainforest vegetation if conditions are right.

On some higher ridges, richer soils derived from the more recent Wianamatta Group overlie the Hawkesbury Sandstone. Where this combines with a higher rainfall zone, such as on the North Shore between Chatswood and Hornsby, forests of tall Blue Gum occur. In the south along the ridge between Sutherland and Cronulla, these shale soils supported Turpentine and Ironbark trees, and in the undisturbed clays of Menai–Lucas Heights grow species with strong affinities to plants of western Sydney. Occasionally, on the edge of the sandstone zone, older red-brown shales of the Narrabeen Group outcrop. A number of species prefer these Narrabeen shales — Forest Oak and Spotted Gum around the shores of Pittwater, and Cabbage Tree Palm and rainforest plants south of Garie Beach through to Palm Jungle in Royal NP.

The west of Sydney is dominated by Wianamatta clay-shale soils. The Turpentine–Ironbark forests from the inner west around Bankstown, Strathfield, Marrickville and surrounds are now largely cleared. Only small remnants of bush or individual old trees remain. Further west are the Cumberland Plains Woodlands, an area bounded in the east by Campbelltown, Bankstown, Parramatta and Castle Hill, and in the west by the Nepean–Hawkesbury River. This is the driest part of Sydney, receiving an average of 800 mm of rain a year compared to 1200–1400 mm along the coast. A number of trees are indicators of this community, notably Narrow-leaved Ironbark, Broad-leaved Ironbark and Grey Box. Specialist clay-loving shrubs include Sickle Wattle, Prickly Parrot-pea, Hairy Bush-pea and Green Bottlebrush. This type of woodland is unique, found nowhere else in Australia, and is regarded as threatened with extinction. Both Federal and State governments have listed it as an 'Endangered Ecological Community'.

One other soil type and floral community deserves a mention, as it supports a fine array of interesting flowering plants. This is the Castlereagh Woodlands, centred on Londonderry, Castlereagh NR and Windsor Downs NR. Here the soils are derived from alluvial sediments — clays, silts, sands and gravel, poor in nutrients. Ironbarks are present, but so too are Hard-leaved Scribbly Gum in sandy areas and Drooping Red Gum in depressions. Of special interest is Agnes Banks NR, just south of Richmond, where sand dunes to 6 m deep have been formed by ancient river deposits and lie like an island surrounded by clays and silts and the extensive Cumberland Plain community to the south and east. Here at Agnes Banks are rare occurrences of Wallum Banksia and Slender Parrot-pea and other plants with close affinities to those on coastal sands.

ABOUT THIS BOOK

This book contains 268 photographs and descriptions. The emphasis is on the common species with conspicuous flowers, but a number of species of localised interest or with striking habit or fruit have also been included, together with the major tree species of the region. Less noticeable plant groups, such as grasses, sedges and ferns, are not included, nor are there many representatives from saltmarsh, wetlands or rainforests. With such a rich diversity from which to choose, there will obviously be omissions, but when you walk along the bushland track or drive along a bush-lined road most of the wildflowers you see should be illustrated in the pages of this book.

An alphabetical layout has been used throughout, with no attempt at botanical grouping. The use of botanical terms has been kept to a minimum, but it is not always possible to describe accurately a plant's features without using specialist terminology. A glossary is provided to explain the botanical terms used.

All photographs have been taken by the author, *in situ*, without flashlight, in an attempt to capture the essential nature of the plant which will aid in identification. Where one species may be confused with another, mention is made under 'Similar species' of simple features which may help distinguish one from another.

Distribution, habitat and flowering times are all based on the author's 30 years experience in observing and photographing Sydney's native plants. Official records of the Royal Botanic Gardens Herbarium have been useful, but if collections are old then plants may in fact be extinct in areas where they were once common, and houses may cover the former bushland habitats. It should be noted that flowering times, whilst a very useful aid to identification, are variable, depending on factors such as weather fluctuations and fire frequency.

Abbreviations

NSW	New South Wales
NT	Northern Territory
NZ	New Zealand
Qld	Queensland
SA	South Australia
Tas	Tasmania
Vic	Victoria
WA	Western Australia
cm	centimetre
diam.	diameter
m	metre
mm	millimetre
ssp.	subspecies
var.	variety
NP	National Park
NR	Nature Reserve
Sanct.	Sanctuary
SRA	State Recreation Area

Family Mimosaceae

Description

Medium tree to 12 m tall with erect or spreading habit and hairy branchlets. Phyllodes lance-shaped or curved, to 10 cm x 2.5 cm, with two conspicuous longitudinal veins. Flower balls pale yellow on an inflorescence shorter than the phyllodes. Seeds borne in straight, flat pod, to 12 cm x 1.5 cm.

Flowering period	Sept. to Nov.
Distribution	Chiefly south of Sydney to Illawarra. Occurs along the coast and tablelands of NSW; also Qld.
Habitat	Sheltered forests, especially on shale and basalt soils, but also on sandy soils on edge of rainforests.
Notes	The name 'binervata' is a reference to the two conspicuous veins in each phyllode.
Similar species	*A. implexa* has several parallel veins in each phyllode.
Specific sites	Waterfall (Royal NP), Appin Road, Darkes Forest.

Family Mimosaceae

Description

Medium to large tree, to 16 m tall, grey-green in appearance, with a rough flaky bark. Branchlets with a fine white pubescence. Phyllodes falcate (sickle-shaped), usually glaucous, about 10 cm x 2 cm, with several longitudinal veins. Flowers in cylindrical heads, to 5 cm long, golden yellow with 1–5 flower heads on a shoot from the base of the phyllodes. Pod narrow and straight, to 5 cm x 0.4 cm.

Flowering period	Sept. to Oct.
Distribution	Scattered throughout Sydney district; also along most of the coast and tablelands zones of NSW.
Habitat	Grows in a diverse range of habitats from eucalypt forest to rocky slopes and along river banks.
Notes	The former name of this species, *A. glaucescens*, described the glaucous or blue-green colour of the phyllodes.
Similar species	None in the region.
Specific sites	Kurnell, Nortons Basin, Carss Park, Rookwood, Sphinx (Ku-ring-gai Chase).

Family Mimosaceae

Description

Spreading prickly shrub usually less than 1 m tall. Phyllodes are straight, rigid, 4-angled and sharp-tipped, about 15 mm long. Flower balls golden yellow with a single flower head in the axil of phyllodes. Pod curved on a thin stalk, to 3 cm x 0.3 cm.

Flowering period	Aug. to Nov.
Distribution	Widespread in the Sydney district and throughout much of NSW; also Qld and Vic.
Habitat	Woodland, heath and scrub, on sandy or clay soils.
Notes	Locally common but inconspicuous when not in flower.
Similar species	*A. ulicifolia* has paler flowers. *A. echinula* has terete, not angular, phyllodes.
Specific sites	Engadine (Royal NP), Oatley Park, Kurnell, Castlereagh NR.

Family Mimosaceae

Description

Medium erect tree, to 15 m tall, with dark almost black bark. Smaller branches have conspicuous raised ridges running along the stem which are often reddish in colour. Leaves bipinnate with 5–12 pairs of pinnae and leaflets openly spaced along pinnae. A gland occurs between each pair of pinnae. Flowers bright golden yellow, with up to 30 flower balls on each inflorescence. Pods straight, flat, to 8 cm x 0.6 cm.

Flowering period	July to Aug.
Distribution	Scattered in Sydney district, but generally absent from Hawkesbury sandstone areas. Mainly a species of Sydney, Blue Mountains and southern NSW. Commonly planted elsewhere in Australia.
Habitat	Open forest and woodland, especially on soils derived from Wianamatta Shale.
Notes	Abundant brilliant yellow flowers make this a conspicuous small tree in western Sydney in mid-winter.
Similar species	*A. parramattensis* has smaller leaflets and flowers in spring and summer.
Specific sites	Bangor–Lucas Heights, Bargo, Castlereagh NR, Scheyville NP.

Family Mimosaceae

Description

Large erect tree, to 18 m tall, with dark fissured bark. Leaves bipinnate, dark green, with 3–5 pairs of pinnae, each pinna with up to 20 pairs of lance-shaped leaflets, about 4 cm long. New foliage is a conspicuous golden colour. Flowers showy, pale yellow, almost white, with up to 50 flower balls on each inflorescence. Pods straight, flat, to 12 cm x 1.2 cm.

Flowering period	Dec. to Feb.
Distribution	Widespread north of Sydney, extending to the Blue Mountains. Commonly cultivated. Also north coast and northern tablelands.
Habitat	Rainforest margin and shaded eucalypt gullies. Frequently planted in regeneration projects.
Notes	One of the tallest wattles in the State.
Similar species	None in the region.
Specific sites	Bents Basin (Nepean River), Upper Lane Cove River, Katandra Res. (Gosford).

Family Mimosaceae

Description

Erect shrub, mostly 1–2 m tall. Phyllodes narrow, straight, rigid, with prominent longitudinal veins, apex with short mucro (sharp point at end of leaf), to 10 cm x 0.4 cm. Flower balls golden yellow, with 1–3 flowers in axils of the phyllodes. Pod straight, flat, to 7 cm x 0.5 cm.

Flowering period	July to Sept.
Distribution	Widespread along coast and western Sydney, extending to Blue Mountains and Southern Highlands. Occurring throughout most of the State; also Vic.
Habitat	Woodland and heath, in both sand and sandy clay, often in damp sites.
Notes	Suitable for cultivation in damp positions or in semi-shade.
Similar species	*A. stricta* has fewer and paler flowers, each borne on short stalks from the leaf axils.
Specific sites	Castlereagh NR, Agnes Banks NR, Windsor Downs NR, Flat Rock Creek (Royal NP).

Family Mimosaceae

Description

Erect open shrub, mostly 2–3 m tall. Branchlets angular and often reddish. Phyllodes falcate and quite large, to 16 cm x 2 cm. Flowers light yellow to almost white, with 11–20 flower balls on an inflorescence from the leaf axils, shorter than the leaves. Pods straight, flat, to 10 cm x 0.8 cm.

Flowering period	April to July.
Distribution	Scattered throughout the Sydney district. Occurring along the coast and northern tablelands of the State; also Qld.
Habitat	Open forest, on clay soils. Absent from sandstone areas.
Notes	Bark contains tannin and was used by Aboriginal people to stupefy fish.
Similar species	None in the region.
Specific sites	Windsor Downs NR, Alfords Point, Lane Cove NP, Castlereagh NR.

Family Mimosaceae

Description

Spreading large shrub or small tree, to 6 m tall, often with pendulous branches. Phyllodes straight, thin, apex acute, with 2–4 prominent longitudinal veins, to 12 cm x 0.8 cm. Flowers yellow in cylindrical heads, grouped in pairs in the axils of phyllodes. Pod straight or curved, flat, to 10 cm x 0.4 cm.

Flowering period	Aug. to Sept.
Distribution	Widespread in the Sydney district. Occurring all along coast and tablelands of the State; also Qld and Vic.
Habitat	Open forest, especially along streams.
Notes	A showy small tree, widely cultivated and used in street planting.
Similar species	*A. longissima* has larger and narrower phyllodes. *A. maidenii* has a golden pubescence on the flower stalk.
Specific sites	West Head picnic area (Ku–ring–gai Chase NP), Bents Basin (Nepean River), Loftus, Bola Creek (Royal NP).

Family Mimosaceae

Description

Medium erect tree, to 10 m tall, with greyish rough bark. Phyllodes falcate, apex rounded-acute, 3–5 prominent longitudinal veins, to 15 cm x 2 cm. Flowers in heads, pale yellow, with 4–8 flower balls on an axillary inflorescence shorter than the phyllodes. Pods conspicuously twisted to 20 cm x 0.5 cm.

Flowering period	Jan. to March.
Distribution	Scattered throughout the Sydney district and most of the State; also Qld and Vic.
Habitat	Open forest and woodland, often on protected slopes.
Notes	Clusters of tangled twisted seed pods are a feature of this species.
Similar species	*A. melanoxylon* has broader more falcate phyllodes and a funicle (seed stalk) which encircles the seed.
Specific sites	Mooney Mooney Creek, Mount Annan, La Perouse, Maroota.

Family Mimosaceae

Description

Erect, slender shrub, mostly 1–2 m tall. Phyllodes narrow, straight, apex acute, to 4 cm x 0.2 cm. Flower heads pale to golden yellow, with 5–9 flower balls on an axillary inflorescence, slightly longer than the phyllodes. Pod woody, straight, flat, to 8 cm x 1.2 cm.

Flowering period	Jan. to April; sporadic flowering at other times.
Distribution	Widespread on sandstone areas of Sydney district, extending to lower Blue Mountains. Also north coast and south coast of NSW.
Habitat	Open forest, woodland and heath, in sandy soils.
Notes	One of the most common small wattles in the area.
Similar species	None in the region.
Specific sites	Oatley Park, Engadine (Royal NP), Devlins Creek (North Epping).

Family Mimosaceae

Description

Large spreading shrub or small tree, mostly 2–4 m tall. Phyllodes straight, with 2–3 longitudinal veins, apex acute, to 15 cm x 2 cm. Flowers golden yellow, in cylindrical heads, with 1 or 2 borne in the axils of phyllodes. Pod straight or curved, cylindrical and up to 10 cm long.

Flowering period	July to Sept.
Distribution	Widespread and common in sandy soils of Sydney district, extending to Blue Mountains and Southern Highlands. Occurring all along coast and tablelands of NSW; also Vic.
Habitat	Open forest, on ridges, slopes and along streams.
Notes	Seeds edible. Often planted in nature strips and local reserves.
Similar species	*A. obtusifolia* begins flowering in December. *A. sophorae* is a decumbent plant of coastal dunes.
Specific sites	Visitor Centre (Royal NP), Kurnell, Waterfall, Lucas Heights.

11

Family Mimosaceae

Description

Erect spreading shrub, mostly 2–4 m tall. Branchlets usually pendulous. Phyllodes long and thin, to 25 cm x 0.5 cm, straight and with an acute apex. Flowers cream, in cylindrical heads, grouped in pairs in axils of phyllodes. Pod straight to curved, cylindrical, dark brown to 10 cm long.

Flowering period	Dec. to Jan., but also sporadic at other times.
Distribution	Mainly occurring in northern suburbs of Sydney. Scattered records along NSW coast and southern tablelands; also Qld.
Habitat	Sheltered forest, usually in gullies or in clay-shale soils.
Notes	A species characterised by its long thin phyllodes and delicate cream flower spikes.
Similar species	*A. floribunda* has broader phyllodes and more abundant flowers.
Specific sites	Lane Cove NP, Maroota-Sackville, Katandra Sanct. (Mona Vale).

Family Mimosaceae

Description

Erect shrub, usually about 1 m tall, with a prostrate form occurring on northern headlands. Stems angular and often reddish. Phyllodes short, broad, with a pointed apex and tending to falcate, to 5 cm x 2 cm. Flower balls pale yellow or almost white, with 2–8 flowers on axillary inflorescence almost as long as the phyllodes. Pod woody, flat, margins undulate, to 7 cm x 0.4 cm.

Flowering period	May to Aug.
Distribution	Widespread and common on sandstone areas of Sydney district. Occurs throughout coast and tablelands of the State; also Qld, Vic, SA, Tas and WA.
Habitat	Open forest and heath, in sandy soils.
Notes	Branchlets of this species are often reddish.
Similar species	None in the region.
Specific sites	Oatley Park, Kurnell, Engadine (Royal NP), Maroota.

13

Family Mimosaceae

Description

Large erect shrub, mostly 2–4 m tall. Phyllodes straight, with 1–3 longitudinal veins, apex blunt or pointed (but not acutely so), to 15 cm x 2 cm. New growth a conspicuous red-tan colour. Flowers yellow to almost white in cylindrical heads, with 2 borne in the axils of the phyllodes. Pod straight, narrow and flat, up to 10 cm long.

Flowering period	Dec. to Feb.
Distribution	Widespread in the Sydney district, extending to Blue Mountains and Southern Highlands. Occurs throughout coast and tablelands of the State; also Qld and Vic.
Habitat	Woodland, in sandy soils, often on sheltered slopes and along streams.
Notes	Young phyllodes are reddish-tan.
Similar species	*A. longifolia* flowers in winter and spring.
Specific sites	O'Hares Creek, Forest Island (Royal NP), Woronora River.

Family Mimosaceae

Description

Erect prickly shrub, mostly 2–3 m tall. Phyllodes rigid, pungent-pointed, with 3–4 longitudinal veins, to 3 cm x 0.5 cm. Flowers golden or pale yellow in cylindrical heads with 1–3 borne in the axils of the phyllodes. Pod straight, cylindrical, sometimes hairy, up to 8 cm long.

Flowering period	July to Oct.
Distribution	Mainly north and north-west of Sydney and in lower Blue Mountains. Also south coast of the State, Vic and SA.
Habitat	Woodland and heath, on exposed sandy plateaux.
Notes	The only Sydney wattle with a combination of pungent phyllodes and flower spikes.
Similar species	None in the region.
Specific sites	West Head (Ku-ring-gai Chase NP), Berowra, Warrah Sanct. (Patonga).

Family Mimosaceae

Description

Medium spreading tree, to 8 m tall, with dark brown to black bark.
Leaves bipinnate with 6–14 pairs of pinnae, each with 20–30 pairs
of closely spaced leaflets. Leaflets are 4–5 mm long and 1 mm wide.
Glands occur between each pair of pinnae and another gland
(known as an interjugary gland) is also found along the leaf rhachis
between one pair of pinnae and the next pair. Young leaves are light
greenish yellow. Flowers golden yellow with 10–20 flower balls on
each inflorescence. Pod straight, flat, to 10 cm long.

Flowering period	Nov. to Feb.
Distribution	Widespread, but especially common in outer Western Suburbs. Occurs all along coast, tablelands and western slopes of NSW.
Habitat	Forest and woodland, usually on clay-shale or the alluvium along streams.
Notes	Once common in the Parramatta district, but has suffered from suburban development.
Similar species	*A. parvipinnula* has silvery bark and branchlets. *A. irrorata* has no glands along the leaf rhachis.
Specific sites	Devlins Creek (Lane Cove NP), Muogamarra NR, Oatley Park, Castlereagh NR.

Family Mimosaceae

Description

Bushy spreading shrub, 2–3 m tall, with soft dense hairs on
branches. Leaves bipinnate with 3–6 pairs of pinnae, each pinna
with 12–20 pairs of leaflets. Leaflets 2–4 mm long. Flowers golden
yellow with up to 25 flower balls on each inflorescence. Pods
straight, flat, red-brown to glaucous, to 5 cm long.

Flowering period	Aug. to Sept.
Distribution	Occurs mainly in western Sydney between Bankstown and Liverpool, with small populations at Menai, Pitt Town and Kemps Creek. Also lower Blue Mountains and north coast of NSW.
Habitat	Open forest, in clay soils derived from Wianamatta shale.
Notes	A threatened species, but being successfully cultivated by local councils for planting in reserves.
Similar species	None in the region.
Specific sites	Rookwood Cemetery, Lansdowne Park, Salt Pan Creek (Bankstown), Longneck Lagoon (Pitt Town).

Family Mimosaceae

Description

Low decumbent shrub, often less than 1 m tall, but may reach 3 m on deep dunes. Phyllodes straight, with 2–4 longitudinal veins, apex acute to obtuse, to 10 cm x 2.5 cm. Flowers golden yellow, in cylindrical heads, with 1 or 2 borne in the axils of phyllodes. Pod straight or curved, terete and up to 10 cm long.

Flowering period	July to Oct.
Distribution	Coast, behind beaches and on sandy headlands. Occurs all along the coastal strip of NSW; also Qld, Vic, SA, and Tas.
Habitat	Coastal sand dunes, sandy scrub and heath.
Notes	A fast growing species used for dune rehabilitation. Formerly regarded as a variety of *A. longifolia*.
Similar species	*A. longifolia* has larger phyllodes and is an erect shrub or small tree.
Specific sites	La Perouse, Towra Point, Kurnell.

Family Mimosaceae

Description

Slender erect shrub, to 2 m tall, with angular branches. Phyllodes straight, narrow, apex acute with a small point, to 12 cm x 0.8 cm. Flower balls pale yellow, enclosed in a set of bracts while in bud; 5–10 flowers on an axillary inflorescence shorter than phyllodes. Pod oblong, flat, to 4 cm x 2 cm.

Flowering period	March to Aug.
Distribution	Widespread and common in sandstone areas of Sydney, extending to Blue Mountains and Southern Highlands. Occurs all along the coast and tablelands of NSW; also Qld, Vic, SA and Tas.
Habitat	Woodland and heath, in sandy soils.
Notes	Flowers of this species are highly scented.
Similar species	None in the region.
Specific sites	Lane Cove NP, Oatley Park, Curra Moors (Royal NP).

Family Mimosaceae

Description

Medium shrub, mostly less than 3 m tall. Leaves bipinnate with up to 6 pairs of pinnae, each pinna with 8–16 pairs of leaflets. Leaflets oblong and 8–12 mm long. Flowers pale yellow with up to 40 flower balls on each inflorescence. Pod oblong, flat, to 10 cm x 1.5 cm.

Flowering period	March to Aug.
Distribution	Widespread on sandstone areas in Sydney district, extending to Blue Mountains and Southern Highlands. Occurring all along coast and tablelands of NSW; also Vic and Tas.
Habitat	Open forest, woodland and scrub, usually on sheltered sandy hillsides.
Notes	A common species with a number of forms.
Similar species	None in the region.
Specific sites	Devlins Creek (North Epping), Kurnell, Curra Moors (Royal NP).

Family Mimosaceae

Description

Prickly shrub, usually less than 1 m tall, although old plants reach 2 m in height. Phyllodes needle-like, crowded, angular, tapering from base to apex, to 14 mm long. Flowers pale yellow, with one flower ball from axil of phyllode on a thin stalk. Pod narrow, often curved, to 5 cm long.

Flowering period	June to Sept.; sporadic flowering at other times.
Distribution	Widespread and common on sandstone areas of Sydney district and throughout much of the State; also Qld, Vic and Tas.
Habitat	Open forest, woodland, heath and sand dunes.
Notes	The common name 'Moses' is derived from 'Mimosa', the original genus of wattles before 1754.
Similar species	*A. brownii* has deeper yellow flower heads. *A. echinula* has terete not angular phyllodes.
Specific sites	Devlins Creek (Lane Cove NP), Castlereagh NR, West Head (Ku-ring-gai Chase NP).

Family Myrtaceae

Description

Attractive tree (4–10 m) with dense glossy foliage. Leaves lance-shaped to broad ovate, upper surface shiny, with numerous oil glands, apex acuminate (tapering to a point), about 8 cm long. Flowers small, creamy-white, in terminal clusters, followed by fleshy round fruits which are white to purple.

Flowering period	Nov. to Feb. Fruits ripen June to Aug.
Distribution	Widespread in the Sydney district, extending to Blue Mountains and Southern Highlands. Occurs along NSW coast, northern tablelands and western slopes; also Qld and Vic.
Habitat	Sheltered gullies, coastal rainforest and protected moist sands.
Notes	An important food plant of rainforest pigeons, rosellas, bower-birds and flying foxes. Fruit also eaten raw by Aborigines.
Similar species	None in the region.
Specific sites	Bobbin Head, Kurrajong, Burning Palms and Upper Causeway (Royal NP).

Family Apiaceae

Description

Slender erect plant, to 80 cm tall, usually an annual but sometimes perennial, with woolly white hairs over most of the plant. Leaves divided into a number of soft segments, to 5 cm long. Flower heads white and showy, 1–2 cm across, surrounded by about 10 petal-like white woolly bracts, giving the impression of a daisy flower. Bracts are often tipped with green. Fruit small, ovate and covered with long hairs.

Flowering period	Mainly Sept. to Jan., but sporadic flowering all year.
Distribution	Widespread and common along coast, adjacent ranges and throughout much of the State; also Qld.
Habitat	Heath, open forest and coastal dunes.
Notes	Germinates rapidly and abundantly after fire.
Similar species	None in the region.
Specific sites	North Head, Kurnell, Oatley Park, Curra Moors (Royal NP).

Family Apiaceae

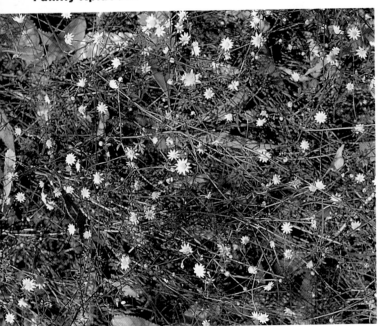

Description

Low perennial, usually straggling through lower vegetation, seldom 50 cm tall. Leaves small, to 8 mm long, divided into 3 segments, with white hairs on the undersurface. Flower heads 4–6 mm across, surrounded by about 10 petal-like white woolly bracts, the entire flower head only 12 mm across. Fruit minute and softly hairy.

Flowering period	Some flowers all year round.
Distribution	Widespread along coast and adjacent ranges; also south coast and southern tablelands of NSW.
Habitat	Open forest, scrub and heath, in sandy soils.
Notes	A common species in the sandstone understorey, but often overlooked because of its small size.
Similar species	None in the region.
Specific sites	Sphinx–Bobbin Head, Devlins Creek (North Epping), Waterfall and Curra Moors (Royal NP).

Family Myrsinaceae

Description

Bushy shrub, to 4 m tall. Leaves alternate, glossy green, entire, obovate, with rounded apex, to 8 cm x 4 cm. Salt crystals are often visible on the upper surfaces of the leaves. Flowers white, bell-shaped and borne in clusters of up to 25, each on a stalk to 1.8 cm long. Fruit a horn-shaped capsule, about 3 cm long, which germinates while still on the plant, maturing in May.

Flowering period	June to Nov.
Distribution	Coastal bays and inlets north and south of Sydney. Occurs along most of NSW coast; also Qld, NT, WA, Pacific Is. and Asia.
Habitat	Tidal mud flats.
Notes	Prefers less salinity than the other Sydney mangrove *(Avicennia)* and is found further up rivers and intertidal creeks.
Similar species	*Avicennia marina*, also a mangrove, has yellow flowers, rounded fruits and breathing tubes in the mud.
Specific sites	Cowan Creek, Lane Cove River, Riverwood wetlands, Oatley Park.

Family Casuarinaceae

Description

Medium to large shrub, often with drooping foliage, to 3 m tall.
Leaves reduced to 6–8 small teeth in whorls around slender
branchlets. Male and female flowers borne on separate plants.
Female flowers small, red, on lateral branches. Male flowers in an
elongated tan spikelet at the end of branches, to 8 cm long. Wind
pollinated. Fruit a woody cone to 3.5 cm long, usually with a
pointed apex.

Flowering period	Female flowers July to Nov. Male flowers May to Oct.
Distribution	Common around Sydney, extending to Blue Mountains and Southern Highlands. Widely distributed along coast and tablelands of NSW; also Vic.
Habitat	Heath and woodland, often dominating scrub near sea, in sandy soils.
Notes	Abundant tan male flowers make this species a conspicuous feature of the bush in winter and early spring.
Similar species	There are 9 species of *Allocasuarina* in the Sydney district and differences between them are small. The large male flower spikes make this species easier to identify.
Specific sites	Kurnell, West Head, North Head, Castlereagh NR, Warrah Sanct. (Patonga).

Family Casuarinaceae

Description

Tree, to 15 m tall, with hard rough bark. Leaves reduced to 6–8 small teeth in whorls around slender branchlets. Male and female flowers usually on separate plants. Female flowers small, reddish, on lateral branchlets; male flowers in spikes at end of branchlets, to 5 cm long. Fruit a woody cone, to 3 cm long, without a pointed apex.

Flowering period	Female flowers April to Oct. Male flowers May to July.
Distribution	Widespread in Sydney district and throughout much of the State. A common and plentiful species, occurring from northern Qld to Tas.
Habitat	Forest, woodland and scrubland, on both ridges and hillsides, in a variety of soils.
Notes	Like all she-oaks, this species is wind pollinated.
Similar species	*A. torulosa* is also tall, but has globular cones.
Specific sites	Heathcote NP, Castlereagh NR, Carss Park, Oatley Park.

Family Casuarinaceae

Description

Shrub, to 2 m tall, with ascending or spreading branches. Leaves reduced to 6–8 small teeth in whorls around slender branchlets. Male and female flowers usually on same plant, but sometimes dioecious. Female flowers small, red, on lateral branchlets; male flowers in spike at end of branchlets, to 2.5 cm long. Wind pollinated. Fruit a woody cone, seldom more than 2 cm long.

Flowering period	Sept. to Feb.
Distribution	Chiefly south of Port Hacking, with isolated populations on northern beaches at Bilgola and Narrabeen Head. Extending to Southern Highlands and south coast; also Vic, SA and Tas.
Habitat	Wet heath and woodland margins.
Notes	The name 'paludosa' is derived from the Latin 'palus', meaning 'marsh' or 'swamp'.
Similar species	Distinguished from other small she-oaks in the area by its swamp habitat and the number of leaf teeth.
Specific sites	Maddens Plain, Curra Moors (Royal NP), Narrabeen Head.

Allocasuarina torulosa   **Forest Oak**

Family Casuarinaceae

Description

Tree, to 25 m tall, with corky bark and slender drooping branchlets.
Leaves reduced to 4–5 small teeth in whorls around branchlets.
Male and female flowers borne on separate plants. Female flowers
red on lateral branchlets; male flowers in spike at end of branchlets,
to 4 cm long. Wind pollinated. Fruit a globular woody cone, flat
topped, to 2.5 cm diameter.

Flowering period	March to Sept.
Distribution	Scattered throughout the Sydney region. Extending along coast and tablelands of NSW; also Qld.
Habitat	Prefers hillsides or tall open forest in richer soils with shale or clay influences.
Notes	Early settlers gave this species the common name of oak as it was used for shingles, flooring and other woodwork.
Similar species	*A. littoralis* can also be a tree, but it does not have globular cones.
Specific sites	Bobbin Head, Scheyville NP, Mitchell Park (Cattai), Bola Creek (Royal NP).

Family Myrtaceae

Description

Large tree, to 30 m tall, with a spreading crown and twisted branches which give this tree its characteristic picturesque appearance. Bark smooth, cream-grey; flakes of bark shed in spring to reveal pink undersurface. Red kino gum often runs down trunk. Leaves opposite, lance-shaped, to 12 cm long. Buds hairy. Flowers abundant, creamy-white, followed by ribbed woody fruit capsules, about 1.2 cm diameter.

Flowering period	Nov. to Dec.
Distribution	Widespread and common on sandstone areas of Sydney district, extending to Blue Mountains. Also north coast and south coast of NSW.
Habitat	Open forest and woodland, on sandstone hillsides or in deep sandy soils.
Notes	For many Sydneysiders, this is the tree which best captures the essence of the Sydney bushland.
Similar species	None in the region.
Specific sites	North Turramurra, Kurnell, Oatley Park, Waterfall, Bents Basin (Nepean River).

Family Myrtaceae

Description

Large tree, to 30 m tall, with a spreading crown and twisted branches. Bark is fibrous, extending to the smaller branches. Leaves opposite, lance-shaped, to 10 cm x 2.5 cm. Flowers creamy-white, followed by ribbed woody fruit capsules, about 9 mm diam.

Flowering period Nov. to Jan.

Distribution Widespread, but usually not in sandstone areas. Occurs throughout much of the State; also Qld and Vic.

Habitat Open forest, often along creek banks in deep alluvial soils or shales.

Notes A species characterised by its crooked branches, fibrous bark and many flowers which attract insects and honeyeaters.

Similar species *A. subvelutina* from the Nepean area has leaves without stalks. *A. bakeri* is a smaller tree with narrower leaves (to 12 mm wide).

Specific sites Bobbin Head, Windsor Downs NR, Scheyville NP, Mt Annan, East Hills Park.

31

Family Myrtaceae

Description

Small twisted or spreading tree, 3–5 m tall, with grey, loose, rough bark. Leaves opposite, broad, stalkless and heart-shaped at the base, to 10 cm long. Buds and new growth covered with reddish-purple hispid hairs. Flowers large with numerous creamy-white stamens, followed by ribbed woody fruit capsules, to 2 cm diameter.

Flowering period	Oct. to Dec.
Distribution	Endemic Sydney species, found on sandstone areas north from O'Hares Creek to Pearl Beach and Putty. Common in coastal national parks.
Habitat	Woodland and heath, in sandy soils.
Notes	Large white flowers attract many native insects, including bees, beetles, flies and moths.
Similar species	None in the region.
Specific sites	Lucas Heights, North Head, Bundeena, Annangrove–Maroota.

Family Fabaceae

Description

Shrub, usually less than 1 m tall. Stems softly hairy, sometimes rust-coloured. Leaves lance-shaped to linear, shiny above, in whorls of 3 or more, margins curved under, to 2 cm long. Flowers bright yellow with a red-brown mark in the centre, borne in upper leaf axils. Calyx with long hairs. Fruit a swollen hairy pod, to 6 mm long.

Flowering period	Aug. to Nov.
Distribution	Coastal sandstone zone south of Broken Bay; also Southern Highlands. Occurring along most of the coast and tablelands of the State; also Qld, Vic and Tas.
Habitat	Woodland and heath, often along creeks in sandy soils.
Notes	The name 'Aotus' means 'without ears', a reference to the lack of bracteoles below the flowers.
Similar species	None in the region.
Specific sites	Kurnell, West Head, Curra Moors (Royal NP).

Family Epacridaceae

Description

Low spreading shrub, seldom more than 50 cm tall. Leaves fine, compact, linear, with entire margins, to 2 cm long. Flowers tubular, red with a yellow and green tip and a tuft of hairs inside near the middle. Fruit a slightly succulent rounded drupe, about 10 mm diameter.

Flowering period	May to Sept.
Distribution	Widespread in sandy areas of the Sydney district and in many areas of the State; also Tas, SA and WA.
Habitat	Woodland and heath, in sandy soils.
Notes	A low shrub with leaves resembling pine needles.
Similar species	A. *humifusum* has flat, narrow-elliptic leaves with toothed margins.
Specific sites	Oatley Park, Wedderburn, Kurnell, La Perouse.

Family Araliaceae

Description

Erect shrub, to 3 m tall, with woolly white hairs covering its branches, inflorescences and lower leaf surfaces. Leaves large, elliptic, entire, with smooth upper surface, to 20 cm x 4 cm. Small white to cream flowers borne on spreading inflorescences, to 60 cm long. Fruit small, compressed and splitting into 2 segments.

Flowering period	Oct. to Jan.
Distribution	Endemic in coastal area north of Sydney Harbour to Gosford and lower Blue Mountains near Winmalee.
Habitat	Forested hillsides, usually near salty inlets, in sandy soils with shale lenses.
Notes	Both the generic and species names refer to the woolly and stellate hairs conspicuous on this plant ('Astron' = star; 'trikhinos' = of hair; 'floccus' = wool).
Similar species	A. *latifolia* does not have a woolly appearance.
Specific sites	Western margins of Pittwater, Bobbin Head–Appletree Bay.

35

Family Avicenniaceae

Description

Large shrub or tree, to 10 m tall, occurring in dense colonies on margins of saltwater estuaries. Leaves opposite, leathery, dark green above, lower surface greyish, to 10 cm x 4 cm. Leaves secrete salt through small glands. Flowers small, orange and in terminal clusters. Fruit a compressed capsule, rounded, 20–25 mm diameter, which germinates on the plant, drops in December and is dispersed by floating.

Flowering period	Feb. to April, but variable. Not flowering every year.
Distribution	Common in tidal zones along coast and estuaries. Extending all along NSW coast; also all mainland States, SE Asia and Pacific Is.
Habitat	Mud flats with tidal inundation. Occasionally on sea rock platforms in sheltered sites.
Notes	The most common mangrove around Sydney. Trees usually surrounded by aerating roots sticking out of the mud.
Similar species	The other mangrove in the area, *Aegiceras corniculatum*, has white flowers and horn-like fruits.
Specific sites	Georges River, Towra Point (Botany Bay), Middle Harbour, Homebush Bay.

Family Myrtaceae

Description

Spreading bushy shrub to small tree, varying in height from 1 m along exposed coast to 10 m or more in rainforest gullies. Bark flaky. Leaves opposite, ovate, pointed, dark green, to 6 cm x 3 cm. Oil glands in leaves distinct. Flowers white with yellow-white sepals and numerous stamens. Fruit a dry one-seeded capsule.

Flowering period	Nov. to Dec.
Distribution	Widespread in the Sydney district. Occurs along coast, tablelands and central west slopes of NSW; also Qld.
Habitat	Margins of streams, especially in shaded sandstone gullies; also rainforest and sea cliff communities.
Notes	A bushy species which may dominate habitats.
Similar species	None in the region.
Specific sites	Upper Hacking River, Bobbin Head, Bola Creek (Royal NP), Scheyville NP.

Family Myrtaceae

Description

Shrub, seldom more than 80 cm tall, with upright rounded leaves, to 5 mm long, which overlap and cover the stems. Flowers 5-petalled, white, solitary and quite small. Petals are only 1.5 mm long. Flowers borne from leaf axils along the upper part of stems.

Flowering period	Nov. to May.
Distribution	Coastal zone north and south of Sydney. Occurs along much of the coast and tablelands of the State; also Qld.
Habitat	Heath and scrub, in sandy soil often in the salt spray zone in rocky headlands, but also away from coast, e.g. Barren Grounds NR.
Notes	The species name 'imbricata' is a reference to the overlapping leaves.
Similar species	None in the region.
Specific sites	Kurnell, Curracurrong (Royal NP), Kangaroo Ck (Royal NP), Maddens Plain.

Family Myrtaceae

Description

Slender shrub, to 2 m tall, often with pendulous branchlets. Leaves linear, with pointed apex, to 15 mm long. Flowers 5-petalled, white, solitary and small. Petals up to 2.5 mm long. Flowers borne on short stalks from leaf axils along the upper part of the branchlets.

Flowering period	Jan. to Feb.
Distribution	Scattered on sandstone areas of coastal zone, extending to Blue Mountains and Southern Highlands. Occurs along much of the coast and tablelands of NSW; also Qld and Vic.
Habitat	Sandstone drip ledges, near waterfalls, wet heaths and creek banks.
Notes	This shrub often has a delicate pendulous habit.
Similar species	None in the region.
Specific sites	Curra Moors Track (Royal NP), Bantry Bay, Devlins Creek (North Epping).

Family Myrtaceae

Description

Prostrate to spreading shrub, to 50 cm tall. Leaves small, opposite, narrow linear, to 10 mm long. Flowers pink, 5-petalled, about 8 mm across, with 10 stamens, borne singly on a slender stalk near the ends of the branchlets.

Flowering period	June to Jan.
Distribution	Widespread on coastal sandstone areas around Sydney. Also north coast of NSW, Vic, SA and Tas.
Habitat	Scrub and open forest, on exposed sandy soil, often with laterite gravels.
Notes	The only species of *Baeckea* in the Sydney district with pink flowers.
Similar species	None in the region.
Specific sites	Curra Moors, Engadine (Royal NP), Lane Cove NP.

Banksia aemula

Family Proteaceae

Description

Large bushy shrub or small tree, to 5 m tall. Leaves leathery, with toothed margins, about 15 cm long and 1.5 cm wide. Flower spikes to 20 cm long, with pale yellow to whitish-green flowers. Pollen presenter on the style conical-ovoid, about 1 mm long, a feature which separates this species from the very similar *B. serrata*. Flower is followed by a thick woody cone containing fruit which open into 2 sections releasing seeds.

Flowering period	Feb. to June.
Distribution	Coastal zone north of La Perouse, with an isolated occurrence at Agnes Banks NR. Also north coast of NSW and Qld.
Habitat	Woodland, in deep sands.
Notes	In Qld, the name 'Wallum' is not only the name of this banksia, but also designates the community in which this species dominates.
Similar species	*B. serrata* has wider leaves and larger (2–3 mm) cylindrical pollen presenter.
Specific sites	Centennial Park, Jennifer Street Res. (La Perouse), Agnes Banks NR.

Family Proteaceae

Description

Large bushy shrub or small tree, to 5 m tall. Leaves small, crowded,
to 10 mm x 1 mm, with margins curled under and a small notch at
the apex. Flower spike to 20 cm long, with orange–red flowers and a
distinctive hooked style. Flower is followed by a thick woody cone
containing fruit which open into 2 sections releasing seeds.

Flowering period	April to Sept.
Distribution	Sandy areas of coast and nearby plateaux of the Sydney district. Extends along most of coast and tablelands of NSW.
Habitat	Woodland and heath, in sandy soils.
Notes	Flowers produce large quantities of honey-like liquid, eagerly sought by honeyeaters; Aborigines also mixed the nectar with water for drinking.
Similar species	None in the region.
Specific sites	Sphinx (Ku–ring–gai Chase), Kurnell, Bundeena–Marley Beach.

Family Proteaceae

Description

A tree of variable height, from almost prostrate in exposed sites to 20 m in protected sites. Leaves narrow elliptic, mostly entire but some irregularly toothed, about 10 cm x 2 cm. Undersurface of leaf is white. Flower spike cylindrical to 12 cm long, with pale yellow flowers. Style straight or curved but not hooked. Flower is followed by a thick woody cone containing fruit which open into 2 sections releasing seeds.

Flowering period	Jan. to July.
Distribution	Mainly coastal, on sandy sites near sea and along estuaries. Occurs all along coast of NSW; also Qld, Vic and Tas.
Habitat	Deep sands and woodlands along tidal inlets.
Notes	Flowers are an important source of nectar for birds. Commonly planted in parks and as a street tree.
Similar species	None in the region.
Specific sites	Bobbin Head, Kurnell, Wattamolla, Oatley Park.

43

Family Proteaceae

Description

Spreading shrub or small tree. Leaves are variable, linear to oblong, either straight or notched at the apex, to 5 cm x 0.8 cm. Leaf margins are mostly entire, but young leaves are sometimes toothed. Flower spike to 8 cm long, with yellow flowers and a straight style. Flower is followed by a thick woody cone containing fruit which open into 2 sections releasing seeds.

Flowering period	Feb. to Aug.
Distribution	Widespread in the Sydney district and throughout much of the State; also Vic, SA and Tas.
Habitat	Open forest and woodland.
Notes	One of the *Banksia* species formerly known as 'honeysuckle' because of its abundant nectar.
Similar species	None in the region.
Specific sites	Darkes Forest, Sphinx (Ku-ring-gai Chase), Engadine, Curra Moors (Royal NP).

Family Proteaceae

Description

Spreading shrub, to 2 m tall. New shoots often with soft rust-coloured hairs. Leaves oblong, with toothed margins, to 8 cm x 2 cm. Main veins on leaf undersurface are covered with velvety rust-coloured hairs when young. Flower spikes to 15 cm long, with pale yellow flowers. Buds are blue-grey in colour. Flower is followed by a thick woody cone containing fruit which open into 2 sections releasing seeds.

Flowering period	March to July.
Distribution	Widespread in sandstone coastal zone of the Sydney district; also north coast of NSW and Qld.
Habitat	Open forest, woodland and heath.
Notes	A rather untidy shrub with conspicuous tan new growth.
Similar species	*B. paludosa* has leaves which narrow gradually to the base. It is mostly hairless, without rust-coloured hairs on new shoots.
Specific sites	Castlereagh NR, Waterfall, Sphinx (Ku-ring-gai Chase), Devlins Creek (North Epping).

Family Proteaceae

Description

Spreading shrub, to 1.5 m tall. Leaves to 8 cm long, toothed on the upper half, wider at the apex and narrowing to the base. Veins on the undersurface yellowish. Flower spikes to 10 cm long, with gold-yellow flowers. Flower is followed by a thick woody cone containing fruit which open into 2 sections releasing seeds.

Flowering period	April to Aug.
Distribution	Southern margins of Sydney to Illawarra and Southern Highlands; also south coast, central tablelands and southern tablelands of NSW.
Habitat	Woodland and heath, in either damp or dry sandy soils.
Notes	Although 'paludosa' infers that this is a swamp-loving plant ('palus' is Latin for 'swamp'), this species is often found on drier slopes and ridges.
Similar species	*B. oblongifolia* has leaves which have rust-coloured hairs on the undersurface.
Specific sites	Curra Moors (Royal NP), Maddens Plain, The Forest Track (Illawarra SRA).

Family Proteaceae

Description

Spreading shrub, to 2 m tall. Branchlets with soft rust-coloured hairs. Leaves large, leathery, toothed, to 25 cm long. Flower spikes to 12 cm long, with greenish-blue flowers turning golden brown with age. Style cream and straight. Flower is followed by a thick woody cone containing fruit which open into 2 sections releasing seeds.

Flowering period	Jan. to July.
Distribution	Scattered on wet sandy areas north and south of Sydney; also north coast of NSW and Qld.
Habitat	Woodland and heath in creek lines and permanently damp sandy sites.
Notes	The name 'robur' (Latin for 'strength') is a reference to the robust habit and large leaves of this species.
Similar species	None in the region.
Specific sites	Goarra Rill (Engadine), Curra Moors (Royal NP), Maddens Plain, Salvation Creek (West Head).

Family Proteaceae

Description

Large shrub or small tree, sometimes 10 m or more tall, but more commonly 3–5 m tall. Leaves leathery, with toothed margins, about 15 cm long and 3–4 cm wide. Flower spike to 16 cm long, with creamy yellow flowers. Pollen presenter cylindrical, 2–3 mm long, a feature which separates this species from the similar *B. aemula*. Flower is followed by a thick woody cone containing fruit which open into 2 sections releasing seeds.

Flowering period	Dec. to June.
Distribution	Widespread in the Sydney district, extending to the Blue Mountains and Southern Highlands. Occurs all along NSW coast; also Qld, Vic and Tas.
Habitat	Open forest, woodland and old sand dunes.
Notes	This is the common, large, gnarled, saw-leaved banksia in the Sydney area.
Similar species	*B. aemula* has narrower leaves and a short (1 mm) conical pollen presenter on the style.
Specific sites	Kurnell, Oatley Park, Devlins Creek (North Epping), Castlereagh NR.

Family Proteaceae

Description

Spreading shrub, to 2 m tall. Leaves narrow, linear, finely toothed near the apex, with margins curled under to conceal most of the white lower surface, to 6 cm long, but only 1–2 mm wide. Flower spikes 15 cm long, with golden yellow to orange flowers and a hooked style which may be yellow or dark red to black. Flower is followed by a thick woody cone containing fruit which open into 2 sections releasing seeds.

Flowering period	March to Sept.
Distribution	Widespread in the Sydney district, extending to the Blue Mountains and Southern Highlands. Occurs all along coast and tablelands of NSW; also Qld and Vic.
Habitat	Open forest, woodland and heath.
Notes	North of Hawkesbury River, this species has a form var. *collina* which has broader toothed leaves.
Similar species	*B. cunninghamii* is a taller shrub with leaves to 5 mm wide and lower surface brownish.
Specific sites	Castlereagh NR, Engadine, Sphinx (Ku-ring-gai Chase).

49

Family Baueraceae

Description

Shrub prostrate to 3 m tall, with many scrambling spreading branchlets. Leaves divided into 3 leaflets, opposite but appearing to be whorls of 6. Leaflets to 12 mm long. Flowers pink with 6–8 petals and 50–60 creamy stamens, borne on stalks longer than the leaves. Flower stalks and sepals hairy.

Flowering period	June to Dec.
Distribution	Widespread in sandy areas of Sydney district, extending to Blue Mountains and Southern Highlands; also southern tablelands of NSW, Qld, Vic, SA and Tas.
Habitat	Creek margins and damp sandy areas in open forest and heath.
Notes	Often forms large thickets along stream banks.
Similar species	*B. microphylla* is a small trailing plant with white flowers.
Specific sites	Heathcote Creek, West Head, Devlins Creek (North Epping).

Family Pittosporaceae

Description

Scrambling plant with twining stems which droop over undergrowth or ascend nearby shrubs. Leaves alternate, variable in shape and hairiness, mostly about 3 cm x 0.6 cm. Flowers cream or greenish yellow, and hang like small bells on short stalks. Berries cylindrical, 2–3 cm long, green, turning brown with age.

Flowering period	Sept. to Dec.
Distribution	Widespread in the Sydney district and in many areas of the State; also Qld, Vic and Tas.
Habitat	Open forest, woodland and heath, especially on hillsides and in gullies.
Notes	Fruits edible raw.
Similar species	None in the region.
Specific sites	Lane Cove NP, Oatley Park, Castlereagh NP, Bents Basin (Nepean River).

Family Blandfordiaceae

Description

Perennial herb, with linear leaves at the base of the stem, to 50 cm long, and 3–10 flowers at the end of an upright stem, usually 60–80 cm tall. Flowers cylindrical, with a red tube about 3 cm long and yellow lobes. Fruit is an erect, 3-angled capsule to 6 cm long.

Flowering period	Nov. to Feb.
Distribution	Widespread along coast north and south of Sydney; also south coast and southern tablelands of NSW.
Habitat	Heath, especially on damp sandy sites.
Notes	The delicate red bells of this species are one of the special delights of the heath around Christmas time.
Similar species	The larger flowered *B. grandiflora* is found north of Hawkesbury River. *B. cunninghamii* is found in the Blue Mountains.
Specific sites	Maddens Plain, Kurnell, Waterfall–Uloola Falls, Wises Track (Royal NP).

Family Rutaceae

Description

Shrub, to 1 m tall. Leaves simple, opposite, narrow elliptic, to 3 cm long, or occasionally divided into 3 leaflets, shiny on upper surface and paler underneath. Flowers bright pink with 4 spreading petals and 8 stamens. Flowers borne singly on a short stalk from leaf axils.

Flowering period	July to Sept.
Distribution	Widespread on sandstone areas in Sydney district. Occurs along south coast and tablelands of NSW; also Vic.
Habitat	Open forest, woodland, and heath.
Notes	One of the most conspicuous and well known wildflowers of the national parks north and south of Sydney.
Similar species	None in the region.
Specific sites	Warrah (Patonga), Sphinx (Ku-ring-gai Chase), Waterfall–Uloola Falls.

Family Rutaceae

Description

Shrub, to 1 m tall. Leaves pinnately divided, with 5–9 leaflets, strongly aromatic when crushed; each leaflet entire and up to 2.5 cm long. Flowers bright pink with 4 petals and borne in loose groups of 3–8 from the leaf axils.

Flowering period	Aug. to Oct.
Distribution	Widespread on sandstone areas north and south of Sydney but more common in the north; also central tablelands and north coast of NSW.
Habitat	Woodland and heath, in sandy soils.
Notes	An attractive shrub with strongly aromatic pinnate leaves.
Similar species	*B. thujona* has 9–13 leaflets, each with rounded teeth; it also has a strong odour when crushed.
Specific sites	Warrah (Patonga), Maroota–Sackville, Sphinx–Bobbin Head.

Family Rutaceae

Description

Shrub, mostly less than 1 m tall, with crowded leaves, broadly ovate, minutely toothed, strongly aromatic and standing upright along the stem. Leaves are about 10 mm x 8 mm. Flowers bright rose-pink and borne in 1–4 flowered clusters at the ends of the branches.

Flowering period	Late Aug. to Nov.
Distribution	Sandstone coastal zone from Wondabyne to Manly and Loftus to O'Hares Creek.
Habitat	Sandy damp heath and rocky sites.
Notes	A well-loved small shrub noted for its brilliant pink terminal flower clusters.
Similar species	None in the region.
Specific sites	Warrah (Patonga), Waterfall–Uloola Falls (Royal NP), O'Hares Creek (Darkes Forest).

Family Fabaceae

Description

Low flat-stemmed straggling shrub, seldom more than 50 cm tall, with leaves apparently absent as they are reduced to minute scales. Stems 4–8 mm wide. Flowers yellow with a red centre, less than 10 mm long, and borne on a short stalk. Small (1 mm) bracteoles occur at or below the middle of this flower stalk, a feature which separates this species from *B. scolopendria*. Fruit a flat pod.

Flowering period	Aug. to Nov.
Distribution	Widespread on sandstone areas of Sydney district. Extending to Blue Mountains and Southern Highlands. Also coast and tablelands of NSW and Qld.
Habitat	Open forest, scrubland and heath, in sandy soils.
Notes	The flat leafless stems are often overlooked when this species is not in flower.
Similar species	*B. scolopendria* has broader stems and larger flowers. *Daviesia alata* also has flat leafless stems, but its orange flowers are in clusters.
Specific sites	Kurnell, Castlereagh NR, Engadine (Royal NP).

Family Fabaceae

Description

Upright small shrub, 50–80 cm tall, with flattened stems. Leaves variable, alternate, ovate to linear, to 25 mm long. Flowers yellow with a dark red keel, to 12 mm long, borne singly on a short stalk from the leaf axils. Fruit a flat pod.

Flowering period	April to July.
Distribution	Widespread and common on sandstone areas of Sydney district. Extending to the Blue Mountains and Southern Highlands. Occurring all along coast, central tablelands and north western slopes of NSW; also Qld.
Habitat	Woodland, in sandy soils.
Notes	The species name is derived from the Greek 'heteros', meaning 'different', and 'phylla', meaning 'leaf', a reference to the variable shape of the leaves on the one plant.
Similar species	*B. stephensonii* has large stipules at the base of each leaf.
Specific sites	Scheyville NP, Oatley Park, Agnes Banks NR, Curra Moors (Royal NP).

Bossiaea obcordata

Family Fabaceae

Description

Erect shrub, seldom more than 80 cm tall, with angular to flattened branches which are spiny-tipped. Leaves alternate, rounded, obcordate (heart-shaped), to 5 mm long. Flowers yellow with red markings, to 8 mm long and are borne on short stalks near the tips of the branches. Fruit a flat pod.

Flowering period	Sept. to Oct.
Distribution	Widespread along coastal zone of Sydney district. Extending to Blue Mountains and Southern Highlands. Also coast and tablelands of NSW, Qld, Vic and Tas.
Habitat	Open forest and woodland, in sandy soils.
Notes	Spine-tipped branchlets are an identifying feature.
Similar species	*B. rhombifolia* lacks the spine-tipped branchlets.
Specific sites	Bents Basin, Sphinx (Ku-ring-gai Chase), Devlins Creek (North Epping), Castlereagh NR.

Family Fabaceae

Description

Erect flat-stemmed shrub, to 1 m tall, with leaves apparently absent as they are reduced to minute scales. Stems to 12 mm wide. Flowers orange-yellow with red centre, 10–14 mm long, borne on short stalk. Small (2 mm) bracteoles occur at or above the middle of the flower stalk, a feature which separates this species from *B. ensata*. Fruit a flat pod.

Flowering period	Aug. to Sept.
Distribution	Coastal sandstone areas around Sydney, but more common north of Sydney Harbour. Extending from Jervis Bay to Somersby (Gosford).
Habitat	Dry woodland and heath, in sandy soils.
Notes	This species is easy to identify because of its broad flat erect leafless stems.
Similar species	*B. ensata* has narrower stems and smaller flowers.
Specific sites	Temptation Creek (West Head), Devlins Creek (North Epping), Muogamarra NR, Poulton Park (Oatley Bay).

Family Fabaceae

Description

Upright small shrub, 60–80 cm tall, with flattened stems. Leaves alternate, elliptic, apex with a fine tip, to 2 cm long. A pair of erect, narrow, triangular stipules, to 10 mm long, occur at the base of each leaf. Flowers yellow with red keel, to 10 mm long, borne singly on a short stalk from leaf axils. Fruit a flat pod.

Flowering period	Aug.
Distribution	Southern area of Sydney between Georges River and Heathcote and north of Sydney in the Brisbane Water NP.
Habitat	Open forest, on ridges and slopes, in sandy soils.
Notes	This species features a pair of large stipules at the base of each leaf.
Similar species	*B. heterophylla* lacks the large stipules at the base of each leaf.
Specific sites	Menai, Heathcote NP, Flat Rock Creek (Royal NP), Engadine, Wondabyne.

Family Epacridaceae

Description

Erect shrub, 30–80 cm tall. Leaves broad lance-shaped to elliptic, 5–12 mm long, paler underneath and with an rounded apex. Flowers white, narrow tubular, 3–4 mm long, and have a ring of hairs inside. A globular fleshy fruit encloses the seeds.

Flowering period	Aug. to Oct.
Distribution	Widespread and common in the Sydney district and throughout much of the State; also Qld, Vic, SA and Tas.
Habitat	Open forest, woodland and heath, in sandy soils.
Notes	Flowers have a strong sweet smell.
Similar species	None in the region.
Specific sites	Agnes Banks NR, Lane Cove NP, Castlereagh NR, Curra Moors (Royal NP).

Family Acanthaceae

Description

Small herb, to 10 cm tall, with tuberous roots. Leaves opposite, elliptic to lance-shaped, to 2 cm long, with lower surface either paler than above or reddish. Flowers blue to mauve, funnel-shaped, with a tube to 10 mm and 5 spreading lobes each 5–8 mm long. Seeds borne in an erect capsule to 15 mm long.

Flowering period	Jan. to March; also Nov., depending on fire.
Distribution	Scattered but uncommon in the Sydney district. Occurs along north and south coast of NSW; also Vic.
Habitat	Woodland and scrubland, in sandy soil.
Notes	This species may be absent from an area for years and re-appear after fire.
Similar species	*B. australis* has larger flowers and hairy leaves.
Specific sites	Pennant Hills, Casula, Castlereagh NR, Oatley Park.

Family Anthericaceae

Description

Grass-like perennial, with tufts of narrow leaves rising from the base of the stem, to 40 cm long. Inflorescence is branched and flowers occur in irregular clusters. They are blue-mauve with darker veins. Filaments are blue with white bands. Fruit is a 3-lobed capsule.

Flowering period	Nov. to Jan.
Distribution	Widespread in the Sydney district, extending to the Blue Mountains. Occurs along coast and tablelands of NSW; also Qld and Vic.
Habitat	Open forest, woodland and heath, in sandy and clay soils.
Notes	A slender perennial which usually goes unnoticed unless in flower.
Similar species	Variety *parviflora* has smaller white flowers.
Specific sites	Picnic Point, Windsor Downs NR, Mt Annan, Scheyville NP.

Family Orchidaceae

Description

Small terrestrial orchid, with a flowering stem to 30 cm tall rising from a solitary prostrate lance-shaped leaf, to 10 cm long. Flowers resemble a flying duck, with a reddish-purple head (lamina) and wings (reflexed sepals). The column forms the duck's body. Flowers are about 2 cm long.

Flowering period	Sept. to Jan.
Distribution	Widespread along coast and adjacent plateaux of Sydney district. Occurs along coast and tablelands of NSW; also Qld, Vic, SA and Tas.
Habitat	Open forest, woodland and heath, in sandy soil.
Notes	The remarkable shape of this orchid is an adaptation to promote fertilisation. The 'head' of the duck is hinged and folds down into the wings when touched.
Similar species	*C. minor* is smaller with a compressed lumpy 'head'.
Specific sites	Agnes Banks NR, La Perouse, Kurnell.

Family Cunoniaceae

Description

Small tree, to 15 m tall, with opposite, broad-lanceolate leaves, to 10 cm long. Leaf margins are distinctly toothed and the undersurface is whitish, in contrast to the shiny green above. Flowers are dull yellow, in round heads like a wattle, on a stalk to 3 cm long. Petals are absent but there are numerous stamens.

Flowering period	Mid-Oct. to Dec.
Distribution	Widespread north and south of Sydney, extending to Southern Highlands and Blue Mountains. Occurs all along coast of NSW and Qld.
Habitat	Damp rocky gullies and banks of sandstone creeks, usually in sheltered situations.
Notes	Branches used by early European settlers for wattle and daub buildings. Blackwattle Bay is named after this species.
Similar species	None in the region.
Specific sites	Middle Harbour, Oatley Park, Bobbin Head, Waterfall.

Family Myrtaceae

Description

Erect or spreading shrub, to 2 m tall. Leaves lance-shaped, to 7 cm long and 6–9 mm wide, with a distinct rigid point. Flowers are bright red in bottlebrush spikes to 10 cm long. These are followed by clusters of small woody fruit, each 5–7 mm diameter.

Flowering period	Late Oct. to Dec.
Distribution	Widespread in the Sydney district and throughout much of the State; also Qld and Vic.
Habitat	Margins of creeks, swamps and wet heaths.
Notes	The common red bottlebrush of wet areas of Sydney.
Similar species	*C. linearifolius* and *C. rigidus* have leaves which are narrower (less than 6 mm wide).
Specific sites	Kurnell, Agnes Banks NR, Sphinx (Ku-ring-gai Chase), Curra Moors (Royal NP).

Family Myrtaceae

Description

Spreading shrub, to 1.5 m tall. Leaves narrow, needle-like or channelled, with a sharp point, to 7 cm long and only 1 mm wide. Flowers lime to yellow-green, in bottlebrush spikes to 7 cm long. These are followed by clusters of small woody fruit.

Flowering period	Sept. to Nov.
Distribution	Chiefly western Sydney; rare in eastern and southern suburbs. Also western slopes of the State.
Habitat	Damp woodland, in clay or shale soils.
Notes	This attractive shrub is becoming uncommon because of urban consolidation.
Similar species	None in the region.
Specific sites	Agnes Banks NR, Castlereagh NR, Kurnell, La Perouse.

Callistemon rigidus **Stiff Bottlebrush**

Family Myrtaceae

Description

Erect or spreading shrub, to 2 m tall, with rigid narrow leaves, to 7 cm long and 3–4 mm wide. Flowers bright red in bottlebrush spikes to 10 cm long. These are followed by clusters of small woody fruit, each 6–7 mm diameter.

Flowering period	Oct. to Nov.
Distribution	Coastal zone north and south of Sydney, but uncommon. Chiefly a Sydney species, but occasionally found elsewhere along coast and tablelands of NSW.
Habitat	Damp scrub, in clay or shale soils, or along sandstone creek lines.
Notes	The botanical name for this species is well chosen: 'calli/stamen' = 'beautiful stamens', 'rigidus' = 'stiff, rigid', a reference to the leaves.
Similar species	*C. linearifolius* has leaves 8–10 cm long and 5 mm wide. *C. linearis* has leaves 1–3 cm wide.
Specific sites	La Perouse, McMasters Beach, Lane Cove NP.

Family Myrtaceae

Description

Erect or spreading shrub, to 2 m tall, with small dense narrow-lanceolate leaves, with a short sharp point, to 4 cm x 0.3 cm. Flowers are red, in bottlebrush spikes to 6 cm long. These are followed by clusters of small woody fruit, each 4–5 mm diameter.

Flowering period	Oct. to March.
Distribution	Restricted in the Sydney district to Woronora River and Heathcote NP. Also occurs on the south coast and southern tablelands of NSW, and Vic.
Habitat	Rocky creek banks.
Notes	The name 'subulatus' refers to the leaf which is narrow and tapers to a fine point.
Similar species	*C. citrinus* has larger leaves, a larger flower spike and a more widespread distribution.
Specific sites	Heathcote Creek, Woronora River (above The Needles).

Calochilus paludosus   **Red Beard Orchid**

Family Orchidaceae

Description

Terrestrial orchid with a sturdy erect flower stem, to 40 cm tall, and a single long basal leaf, to 18 cm x 0.5 cm. Stems carry up to 8 flowers. Flowers with conspicuous bearded labellum, at least 2 cm long, covered with shiny red hairs. Sepals and petals green, with reddish veins. Above the beard is a cup-like collar flanking the stigma. A prominent coloured ridge connects both sides of the collar, but this species is without the dark glands that are present in other *Calochilus* in the region.

Flowering period	Sept. to Nov.
Distribution	Scattered but uncommon along the coastal zone; extending into the Blue Mountains. Occurs throughout most of eastern Australia; also Tas and NZ.
Habitat	Heath and woodland, in both swampy and dry sandy conditions.
Notes	Despite the name 'paludosus', around Sydney this plant is more likely to be found in dry woodland beneath eucalypts.
Similar species	*C. campestris* has a beard coloured metallic blue and purple. *C. robertsonii* has a shiny purple to bronze beard.
Specific sites	Castlereagh NR, Oatley Park, Brisbane Water NP.

Family Myrtaceae

Description

Spreading often dense shrub, to 2 m tall, with small crowded leaves, to 8 mm long. Flowers with 5 white to pink starry petals and numerous protruding stamens, arranged in showy terminal heads. As flowers fade, sepals develop long reddish-purple awns up to 15 mm long which are a conspicuous feature of the plant throughout summer.

Flowering period July to Oct.

Distribution Widespread on sandstone areas of Sydney district and throughout much of the State; also Qld, Vic, SA, Tas and WA.

Habitat Scrub and heath, in sandy soils.

Notes A showy species with abundant flowers followed by colourful enlarged sepals.

Similar species None in the region.

Specific sites West Head, La Perouse, Lucas Heights, Curra Moors (Royal NP).

71

Family Asteraceae

Description

An upright shrub, to 2 m tall, with stems and upper leaf surfaces covered with minute glandular hairs. Leaves narrow-elliptic, flat, to 5 cm long, and paler below. Brilliant golden-yellow flowers are borne in dense terminal clusters, each up to 12 cm across.

Flowering period	Oct. to Dec.
Distribution	Scattered around Sydney, but not common. Occurs all along the NSW coast; also Blue Mountains.
Habitat	Woodland and open forest, especially on sheltered slopes, in sandy soil.
Notes	The large shiny gold flower heads are aptly named, as 'aurum' is Latin for 'gold' and 'niton' is Latin for 'shine'.
Similar species	*C. denticulata* has creamy-yellow flower heads and small (2 cm) leaves.
Specific sites	Waterfall, Little Salt Pan Creek, Oatley Park, Thirlmere Lakes.

Family Casuarinaceae

Description

Tree with drooping branchlets, to 20 m tall. Leaves reduced to
12–16 small teeth in whorls around the slender branchlets. Male
and female flowers borne on separate plants. Female flowers small
and red, on lateral branchlets; male flowers in a dense elongated
spike at end of branchlets. Wind pollinated. Fruit a woody cone to
2 cm long.

Flowering period	June to Aug.
Distribution	Scattered along coastal estuaries and larger creeks of western Sydney; also north coast, south coast and central western parts of the State, and Qld.
Habitat	Estuarine flats, often behind mangroves, and along slow moving creeks.
Notes	This species is long lived and is commonly used in landscaping.
Similar species	*C. cunninghamiana* has 8–10 leaf-teeth and is restricted locally to flood plains and river flats on the margins of Sydney.
Specific sites	Mona Vale, Olympic Park (Homebush Bay), Oatley Park, Scheyville NP.

Family Cunoniaceae

Description

Small tree, to 5 m tall. Leaves opposite, divided into 3, each leaflet lance-shaped, toothed and 3–6 cm long. Abundant white flowers are borne in branched inflorescences. As the fruit forms, the calyx turns pink to red and enlarges from about 2 mm to 12 mm, forming the coloured 'flowers' which are sold in bunches around Christmas time.

Flowering period	Late Oct. to Nov. Red sepals in Dec. and Jan.
Distribution	Widespread in sandy areas of Sydney district, extending to Blue Mountains and Southern Highlands; also north coast and south coast of NSW.
Habitat	Forest and woodland, usually in sheltered locations in deep sandy soil.
Notes	A well-known plant, often grown in suburban gardens. Some cultivated forms have deep red 'flowers'.
Similar species	None in the region.
Specific sites	Kurnell, Oatley Park, North Turramurra–Bobbin Head.

Family Chloanthaceae

Description

Low straggling shrub, seldom more than 40 cm tall, with a woolly appearance. Leaves narrow, to 4 cm long, very wrinkled on the upper surface and with margins bent under to almost cover the white woolly undersurface. Flowers yellowish-green, tubular, hairy, borne singly from leaf axils and longer than the leaves.

Flowering period July to Oct.

Distribution Widespread in sandy areas of Sydney district, extending to Blue Mountains. Also north coast, south coast and central western slopes of NSW, Qld and WA.

Habitat Rocky slopes in woodland, scrubland and heath.

Notes A low plant, often overlooked because of its yellow-green flowers.

Similar species *C. glandulosa* has glandular hairs on the leaves. It is restricted to lower Blue Mountains.

Specific sites Bobbin Head, Narrabeen, O'Hares Creek (Darkes Forest), Curracurrong (Royal NP).

Family Fabaceae

Description

Small undershrub, to 50 cm tall, with narrow alternate leaves which
have a hooked or pointed apex, are pubescent underneath and up
to 25 mm x 3 mm. Yellow pea flowers are borne on a slender
inflorescence and are followed by a swollen pod, about 6 mm diam.

Flowering period	Sept. to Dec.
Distribution	Scattered in western suburbs of Sydney, mainly in clay areas. Threatened by urban spread.
Habitat	Woodland and grassland in clay soils derived from Wianamatta shales and sandy alluvium.
Notes	The eastern representative of a genus much more common in Western Australia.
Similar species	None in the region.
Specific sites	Narellan, Lansdowne Park, Windsor Downs NR, Scheyville NP.

Family Vitaceae

Description

Large climbing plant, becoming very woody with age and growing by means of tendrils over understorey or into higher canopy of rainforest trees. Leaves divided into 5 broad leaflets to 10 cm long, glossy green above and glaucous underneath. Flowers small, yellow and borne in terminal umbels, followed by grape-like bunches of purple-black fruit.

Flowering period	Nov. to Dec.
Distribution	Widespread in the Sydney district and along coastal and tablelands zones of NSW; also Qld and Vic.
Habitat	Rainforest and shaded slopes and gullies.
Notes	*Cissus* belongs to the same family as cultivated grapes, a similarity which can be seen in the fruits.
Similar species	*C. sterculiifolia* has glands in the main veins of the leaf. It is rare.
Specific sites	Barrenjoey Head, Bobbin Head, Kurnell, Bola Creek (Royal NP).

77

Family Ranunculaceae

Description

Vigorous climber which drapes itself over understorey and small trees. Leaves are in groups of 3, ovate, thin, entire or with a few teeth, to 8 cm x 4 cm. Flowers white with 4 spreading petal-like sepals and numerous yellow stamens. Fruit develop long beard-like appendages which are as attractive and conspicuous as the flowers.

Flowering period	Aug. to early Oct.
Distribution	Widespread in the Sydney district and in many areas of the State; also Qld and Vic.
Habitat	Forests, usually on sheltered slopes.
Notes	The common name is a reference to the conspicuous fruit which has fluffy appendages.
Similar species	*C. aristata* has firmer leaves and a 1 mm appendage on each anther.
Specific sites	Bobbin Head, Lime Kiln Bay (Oatley), Mt Annan, Bola Creek (Royal NP).

Clerodendrum tomentosum   **Hairy Clerodendrum**

Family Verbenaceae

Description

Large shrub or small tree, to 5 m tall, with a soft hairy appearance.
Leaves opposite, broadly ovate, pubescent to 12 cm x 3.5 cm.
Flowers creamy, with a thin tube to 2 cm long, 5 spreading lobes
and 4 stamens which protrude from the tube. These are followed by
conspicuous purple-black succulent fruit which sit on the red fleshy
calyx.

Flowering period	Late Oct. to Nov.
Distribution	Scattered along coastal zone of Sydney district. Occurs along coast, tablelands and central western slopes of NSW; also Qld and WA.
Habitat	Protected sites in sandstone soils, and rainforest margins.
Notes	Softly hairy leaves, distinctive tubular flowers and colourful fruit make this species unmistakable.
Similar species	None in the region.
Specific sites	Razorback Mt., Patonga, Oatley Park, Bola Creek (Royal NP).

79

Family Polygalaceae

Description

Slender erect shrub, to 1 m tall, often with reddish stems. Leaves small, linear, to 15 mm long, with margins which curl under. Numerous pink flowers are borne at the ends of the stems. Flowers have spreading ear-like sepals. Fruit is a compressed capsule, about 7 mm long, which stands upright.

Flowering period	Sept. to Dec.
Distribution	Widespread in the Sydney district and in many areas of the State; also Qld, Vic, SA and Tas.
Habitat	Woodland, scrubland and heath, in sandy soils.
Notes	Flowers resemble match heads when in bud, but develop two winged sepals when in flower which create the appearance of a pea flower.
Similar species	None in the region.
Specific sites	Castlereagh NR, Agnes Banks NR, Oatley Park, Curra Moors (Royal NP).

Family Polygalaceae

Description

Lax low-growing plant, seldom more than 15 cm tall, with straggling leafless stems. Bright blue flowers grow on stems up to 9 cm long. These flowers are 5–8 mm long and have ear-like wing sepals about 6 mm long. Flowers are followed by flattened spherical capsules.

Flowering period	Oct. to March.
Distribution	Widespread in the Sydney district, but never common. Extending all along the coast and tablelands of NSW.
Habitat	Woodland and heath, in sandy soils and alluvium.
Notes	This leafless plant is usually unnoticed in the lower understorey unless it is in flower.
Similar species	*C. defoliatum* is taller; its flowers are smaller and its fruit is ovate and narrowing to the base.
Specific sites	West Head, Lane Cove NP, Agnes Banks NR, Castlereagh NR.

Family Proteaceae

Description

Erect shrub with slender ascending branches, to 80 cm tall. Leaves crowded, upright, linear, almost needle-like, to 15 mm long and only 1 mm wide. White flowers produced in showy heads on long stalks. Each flower small, tubular and with an upper lobe broader than 3 lower lobes. Fruit cone-shaped, small dry, 2–3 mm long, crowned with a ring of hairs.

Flowering period	July to Oct.
Distribution	Coastal zone north of Sydney to near Wyong; also Jervis Bay area of south coast.
Habitat	Woodland and heath, in sandy soils.
Notes	This species intergrades with *C. taxifolium* and is sometimes regarded as a narrow leaf form of that species.
Similar species	*C. taxifolium* has flat, wider, twisted leaves. *C. ellipticum* has broader elliptic leaves and occurs south of Sydney.
Specific sites	Warrah Sanct. (Patonga), Mt Colah–Bobbin Head.

Conospermum longifolium ssp. *angustifolium*

Family Proteaceae **Long-leaf Coneseeds**

Description

Erect shrub with slender ascending branches, to 1.5 m tall. Leaves
long and narrow, to 25 cm long but less than 4 mm wide. White
flowers produced in showy heads on stalks up to 20 cm long and
held high above the leaves. Each flower small, tubular and with an
upper lobe broader than the 3 lower lobes. Fruit cone-shaped, small
dry, 2–3 mm long, crowned with a ring of hairs.

Flowering period	July to Nov.
Distribution	Restricted to southern part of Sydney, between Georges River and Appin. Other subspecies are more widespread.
Habitat	Open forest, woodland and heath, in sandy soils.
Notes	A very variable species with a number of different leaf forms.
Similar species	Subspecies *longifolium* has broader lance-shaped leaves; it occurs north of Sydney Harbour.
Specific sites	Engadine, Curra Moors (Royal NP), O'Hares Creek (Darkes Forest).

83

Family Rutaceae

Description

Low to medium compact shrub, mostly less than 1 m tall, with thick, round to ovate leaves, white hairy underneath, to 3 cm long. Flowers star-like, white, with 4 petals and 8 stamens, borne in small clusters at the ends of the branchlets.

Flowering period	May to Sept.
Distribution	Scattered along the coastline near the sea. Occurs all along the NSW coast; also Vic and Tas.
Habitat	Rocky and sandy margins of the sea.
Notes	Tolerant of salt spray and a useful garden plant for coastal suburbs.
Similar species	None in the region.
Specific sites	Kurnell, La Perouse, Marley Beach (Royal NP).

Family Rutaceae

Description

Spreading to erect shrub, usually less than 1 m tall, with opposite, ovate leaves, to 4 cm x 2 cm. Flowers tubular, to 3 cm long, with 4 spreading petals and 8 stamens which extend beyond the tube. Flowers may be red with green tips or completely yellowish-green. The red flower is usually more inflated; the green flower is narrower.

Flowering period	May to Sept.
Distribution	Widespread on sandstone areas in Sydney district and in many areas of the State; also Qld, Vic, SA and Tas.
Habitat	Open forest, woodland and heath, in sandy soils.
Notes	Cultivars of this species are widely grown in native gardens and its flowers have long been used as motifs to decorate objects.
Similar species	None in the region.
Specific sites	Oatley Park (green form), Woronora River (green form), Curra Moors Track, Royal NP (red form).

Family Myrtaceae

Description

Medium to large tree, to 20 m tall, or sometimes a mallee with
lignotuber on heath. Bark rough, fibrous, with a distinctive
tessellated appearance, covering the entire tree. Trunk often exudes
red kino gum. Leaves lance-shaped, to 15 cm x 3 cm. Flowers white
and borne in dense terminal clusters. Fruit capsules are urn-shaped
and are found in abundance beneath the tree.

Flowering period	Feb. to April.
Distribution	Widespread and common in the Sydney district, extending to Blue Mountains and Southern Highlands. Occurs along most of coast and tablelands of NSW; also Qld and Vic.
Habitat	Forest, woodland and heath, on exposed ridges and upper slopes, in sandy soil.
Notes	The name 'gummifera' refers to the abundant red gum or sap exuded from the trunk.
Similar species	None in the region.
Specific sites	Kurnell, Castlereagh NR, Oatley Park, Sphinx (North Turramurra).

Family Myrtaceae

Description

A handsome tall straight tree, to 30 m tall, which mostly occurs in pure stands. Bark smooth and shed in flakes to produce a spotted effect. Leaves lance-shaped, to 20 cm x 2.5 cm. Flowers creamy-white, in groups of 3 and borne in dense terminal clusters. Fruit capsules are urn–shaped.

Flowering period	March to May, but not every year.
Distribution	Scattered and localised in the Sydney district. Occurs along NSW coast, central tablelands and central western slopes; also Vic.
Habitat	Open forest, in clay and shale soils. Not found on Hawkesbury Sandstone.
Notes	Both Cumberland Plain Woodland and Pittwater Forest where this species occurs are listed as Endangered Ecological Communities.
Similar species	None in the region.
Specific sites	Towler Bay (West Pittwater), Avalon, Cecil Park, Appin, Bents Basin.

Family Rutaceae

Description

Small slender shrub, to 80 cm tall, with glabrous, angled branches
and alternate, narrow-elliptic leaves, to 5 cm long. Flowers pink, 5-
petalled, about 25 mm across, with 10 hairy stamens arranged like a
cage around the ovary. Flowers are borne along the stem from the
leaf axils.

Flowering period	Feb. to June.
Distribution	Endemic to coastal sandstone zone north and south of Sydney.
Habitat	Open forest, on sheltered sandy sites.
Notes	The name 'saligna' is a reference to the supposed willow-like leaves ('Salix' = 'willow').
Similar species	*C. exalata* has smaller leaves and terete branchlets.
Specific sites	Manly Dam, Curra Moors (Royal NP), Robertson Track (Royal NP).

Family Rhamnaceae

Description

Small tough shrub, to 80 cm tall, with short side branches which are often spiny. Leaves small, elliptic, 2–5 mm long. Flowers white, bell-shaped, covered with soft hairs and only 2–4 mm long. They are scattered along the stem or in clusters at the ends of the branches.

Flowering period	June to Aug.
Distribution	Widespread in Sydney district and throughout much of the State; also Qld, Vic, SA and Tas.
Habitat	Open forest, woodland and heath, in sandy soil.
Notes	Although the flowers of this species are small, they are very conspicuous in winter when little else is in flower.
Similar species	*C. ericoides* bears its flowers in dense terminal heads. *C. spinescens* has its flowers hairless at the base and softly hairy on the top half.
Specific sites	Castlereagh NR, Oatley Park, Curra Moors (Royal NP).

Family Orchidaceae

Description

Terrestrial orchid with broad lance-shaped leaves, to 12 cm x 3 cm,
dark green above, purplish below. Flowering stems erect, 20–50 cm
tall, bearing up to 12 flowers. Labellum erect and broad, to 3 cm
long, forming a hood which is green with conspicuous purple
stripes and spots. The hood is backed by narrow spreading green
sepals and petals.

Flowering period	Dec. to Feb.
Distribution	Widespread along coast, extending to Blue Mountains. Occurs all along coast of NSW; also Vic.
Habitat	Heath, woodland and open forest, in sandy soil, often at the base of large eucalypt trees.
Notes	Usually found in small colonies. This orchid is easily recognised because of its distinctive upright hood.
Similar species	*C. subulata* has a flower resembling a cow's head with two 'horns' spreading above the flower.
Specific sites	Pennant Hills Park, Poulton Park (Oatley Bay), Garrawarra (Royal NP).

Family Sapindaceae

Description

Small to large spreading tree, to 20 m tall, with a large compound leaf divided into 6–10 leaflets, which are obovate, to 12 cm x 5 cm. Leaflets are leathery and notched at the apex. Flowers small, whitish-yellow and borne in long clusters. These are followed by 3-lobed orange fruit.

Flowering period	Feb. to July.
Distribution	Scattered along coastline north and south of Sydney, near the sea or estuaries; also north coast of NSW and Qld.
Habitat	Sheltered scrub and littoral rainforest, on dunes.
Notes	A stunted tree along Port Hacking where it is close to the southern limit of its range.
Similar species	None in the region.
Specific sites	Nielsen Park, Towra Point, Jibbon Beach (Bundeena).

Cymbidium suave

Family Orchidaceae

Description

Epiphytic orchid, forming clumps in hollow limbs and between tree branches. Leaves narrow, strap-like, upright or drooping, to 40 cm long. Flowers numerous along a stem to 30 cm long, golden green with blotches of yellow and red.

Flowering period	Oct. to Dec.
Distribution	Scattered throughout Sydney district. Chiefly found along coastal areas of NSW, but extending in places to tablelands; also Qld.
Habitat	Moist forests or sheltered woodlands, on tree branches and in hollows.
Notes	Often mistaken for a sedge when not in flower. Commonly grown in native gardens.
Similar species	None in the region.
Specific sites	Castlereagh NR, Curra Moors Track (Royal NP), Walumarra Track (Royal NP).

Family Goodeniaceae

Description

Erect or spreading small shrub, to 50 cm tall, with angular hairless stems. Leaves narrow-elliptic, often with a few broad teeth, to 3 cm long. Flowers blue, irregular in shape, to 2 cm long, with a yellow throat and rust-coloured hairs on the back.

Flowering period	July to Dec.
Distribution	Widespread on sandstone areas of Sydney district. Occurs all along coast and tablelands of NSW; also Qld, Vic and Tas.
Habitat	Open forest, woodland and heath, in sandy soil.
Notes	The name 'stricta' is a reference to the upright habit of this species.
Similar species	*D. purpurea* has purple flowers and brown hairs on the flowering stems.
Specific sites	Sphinx–Bobbin Head, Waterfall–Uloola Falls, Devlins Creek (North Epping).

Family Myrtaceae

Description

Small spreading shrub, to 80 cm tall, with crowded compressed leaves, to 10 mm long x 1 mm wide. Flowers white, in heads of 2–4, with a short floral tube, to 5 mm long, and a white style protruding beyond the tube. Flowers may develop a pink hue as they mature.

Flowering period	Sept. to Dec.
Distribution	Restricted to two areas of Sydney: Loftus–Royal NP–O'Hares Creek and Terrey Hills–Forestville.
Habitat	Woodland and heath, in sandy soils.
Notes	This plant is on the national rare species list because of its localised distribution.
Similar species	*D. biflora* has flowers in pairs. *D. grandiflora* is more prostrate and has larger flowers.
Specific sites	Waterfall (Royal NP), Anise Falls (Royal NP), Lucas Heights, Heathcote NP.

Family Myrtaceae

Description

Erect multi-branched shrub, to 1.5 m tall, with crowded, needle-like leaves, to 15 mm long. Flowers in clusters of 4–20, white and pink on the same plant. Flower tube to 7 mm long with a straight style, about 12 mm long, protruding beyond the tube.

Flowering period	June to Sept.
Distribution	Restricted to the coastal zone between Brisbane Water NP and Bulli.
Habitat	Heath, in exposed sandy soils.
Notes	Genus named after Erasmus Darwin, grandfather of naturalist Charles Darwin. 'Fascicularis' refers to the bundle of flowers similar to Roman 'fasces', a bundle of rods with axe in the middle.
Similar species	None in the region.
Specific sites	Kurnell, Waterfall–Uloola Falls, West Head, Warrah Sanct. (Patonga).

Family Myrtaceae

Description

Erect shrub, usually 1–2 m tall, with crowded compressed leaves, to
25 mm long. Flowers in clusters of 4, mostly white but turning pink
with age. Flower tube to 8 mm long, with a straight white style, to
20 mm long, protruding beyond tube.

Flowering period	July to Oct.
Distribution	Restricted to a narrow band between Middle Harbour and Gosford.
Habitat	Sheltered open forest, especially along creeks.
Notes	An attractive erect shrub and a local endemic recorded on the national rare species list.
Similar species	None in the region.
Specific sites	Bobbin Head, Jerusalem Bay, Middle Harbour Creek (Garigal NP).

Family Fabaceae

Description

Prostrate shrub with flat winged leafless stems, to 5 mm wide. Groups of 2–5 pea flowers occur along the stems. These are orange with deep red centres and are followed by small triangular pods.

Flowering period	Aug. to Nov.
Distribution	Widespread but uncommon in sandstone areas of Sydney district. Also occurring along the coast and tablelands of NSW.
Habitat	Open forest and woodland, in sandy soil.
Notes	The unusual prostrate habit, orange flowers and leafless flat stems make this an easy species to identify.
Similar species	*Bossiaea ensata* also has flat leafless stems, but its flowers are yellow and borne singly.
Specific sites	Lucas Heights, Manly, Castlereagh NR, Budderoo NP.

Family Fabaceae

Description

Upright multi-branched shrub, to 2 m tall, with obovate leaves, to 6 cm x 2 cm. A network of small veins is prominent on each leaf. Flowers small, but abundant, yellow with a red centre and crowded at the ends of long thin flower stalks. Pod is small and triangular.

Flowering period	Sept. to Nov.
Distribution	Widespread in the Sydney district, extending to Blue Mountains, Southern Highlands and Nowra. Also north coast and south coast of NSW.
Habitat	Open forest and woodland, in sandy soil.
Notes	The name 'corymbosa' is a reference to flowers being borne in a corymb, an arrangement where flowers are at the same level even though the flower stalks begin at different levels.
Similar species	None in the region.
Specific sites	O'Hares Creek (Darkes Forest), Oatley Park, Thirlmere Lakes, Maroota.

Family Fabaceae

Description

Erect prickly shrub, to 1.5 m tall, with short rigid branchlets ending in a spine and narrow pungent leaves, to 12 mm long. Flowers yellow with dark red centre, solitary or 2–4 on a short stalk. Pod small and triangular.

Flowering period	Aug. to Sept.
Distribution	Widespread in the Sydney district and throughout much of the State; also Qld, Vic, SA, Tas and WA.
Habitat	Open forest, woodland and scrubland, in both sandstone and shale soils.
Notes	A spiny shrub with leaves resembling the European gorse (*Ulex*).
Similar species	None in the region.
Specific sites	Windsor Downs NR, Castlereagh NR, Scheyville NP, Bents Basin (Nepean River).

Family Orchidaceae

Description

Large showy rock-loving orchid, to 80 cm tall, with smooth leathery leaves rising from swollen stem bases, to 25 cm long and 6 cm wide. Flowers white to dull yellow, almost 4 cm across, with up to 100 flowers borne along an inflorescence to 50 cm long.

Flowering period	Aug. to Sept.
Distribution	Scattered along coastal zone of Sydney district; also Vic.
Habitat	Sheltered rocks in moist protected forests.
Notes	A common orchid in native gardens. Pseudo-bulbs can be eaten, but contain little nutrition. The most spectacular of the local orchids.
Similar species	None in the region.
Specific sites	Warrah Sanct. (Patonga), Bents Basin (Nepean River), Palm Jungle (Royal NP).

Family Phormiaceae

Description

Perennial, with long flat leaves, to 60 cm x 2 cm, which may rise in tufts from ground level, or, in variety *producta*, from an elongated stem. Leaves are folded and fused near the base and usually have sandpapery margins and keel. Flowers with 6 blue-mauve segments are borne above the leaves on an upright stem to 50 cm long. Stamens have a yellow swelling and pale yellow-brown anthers. Fruit is a blue-purple berry.

Flowering period	Oct. to Feb.
Distribution	Widespread in the Sydney district and in many areas of the State; also Qld, Vic and Tas.
Habitat	Open forest, woodland and heath, in sandy soils.
Notes	A species with a number of named varieties in the Sydney district. All have blue flowers and blue-purple berries.
Similar species	*D. revoluta* has leaves more than half folded and fused and brown-black anthers. *D. longifolia* has pale blue flowers and yellow anthers.
Specific sites	Mt Annan, Oatley Park, Bents Basin (Nepean River).

Family Anthericaceae

Description

Erect perennial, with long grass-like leaves in a clump at the base of the plant. Flower stems 30–60 cm tall; they bear clusters of 2–4 pendulous flowers, which have pink-mauve petals and 6 deep purple stamens. Fruit a cylindrical capsule, to 7 mm long, surrounded by persistent old flowers.

Flowering period	Nov. to Dec.
Distribution	Scattered and uncommon in the Sydney district. Chiefly a species of the tablelands and western slopes and plains; also Qld, Vic, SA and WA.
Habitat	Grassland and woodland, often on clay soils.
Notes	Flowers have a chocolate scent.
Similar species	*D. strictus* has only one flower per node.
Specific sites	Doonside, Mt Annan, Scheyville NP.

Dillwynia floribunda var. floribunda Flowery Parrot-pea

Family Fabaceae

Description

Erect shrub, to 2 m tall, with crowded, twisted, warty, linear leaves, to 15 mm long. Flowers yellow with red centre; they occur in pairs usually closely packed along the upper branches, often extending 15–25 cm down the branches. Pod rounded, inflated, to 6 mm long.

Flowering period	July to Oct.
Distribution	Sandy coastal areas around Sydney, extending to adjacent plateaux. Occurs all along NSW coast to Qld.
Habitat	Heath and woodland, in wet sandy soils.
Notes	The long yellow flower spikes of this species may dominate suitable swampy habitats.
Similar species	*D. floribunda* var. *teretifolia* has more terete, less warty leaves and grows in drier soils (e.g. Castlereagh NR, Mitchell Park). *D. retorta* has flowers which are not packed closely together.
Specific sites	Lucas Heights, Manly, Waterfall, Curra Moors (Royal NP).

Family Fabaceae

Description

Erect or spreading shrub, to 2 m tall, with twisted, linear leaves, to 12 mm long. Flowers yellow with a red centre. On some plants, flowers are borne on very short stalks in loose clusters near the ends of branchlets; on other plants flowers are in inflorescences with stalks to 2 cm long. Pods round, inflated, to 6 mm long.

Flowering period	June to Nov.
Distribution	Widespread in the Sydney district, extending to Blue Mountains. Occurring all along coast and central tablelands of the State; also Qld.
Habitat	Woodlands and heath, chiefly in sandy soils.
Notes	The most common of the yellow and red pea-flowers known as 'eggs and bacon'. A very variable species.
Similar species	*D. floribunda* has flowers from leaf axils near the top of stems. *D. glaberrima* has leaves which are not spirally twisted.
Specific sites	La Perouse, Castlereagh NR, Waterfall–Uloola Falls, Oatley Park.

Dillwynia sieberi   **Prickly Parrot-pea**

Family Fabaceae

Description

Rigid, erect shrub, to 1.5 m tall, with small needle-like leaves, grooved on the upper surface, finely pointed, to 15 mm long. Flowers yellow with red centre, backed by a softly hairy calyx. Flowers borne at the ends of short side branchlets. Pod rounded, inflated, to 6 mm long.

Flowering period	Sept. to Nov.
Distribution	Western Sydney in clay areas, extending south-west to Southern Highlands. Scattered throughout much of the State; also Qld.
Habitat	Open forest, woodland and scrub, in clay soils derived from Wianamatta Shale.
Notes	Formerly classified as *D. juniperina*, a reference to its sharp juniper-like leaves.
Similar species	None in the region.
Specific sites	Rookwood Cemetery, Castlereagh NR, Windsor Downs NR.

Family Fabaceae

Description

Weak shrub, seldom more than 80 cm tall, with softly hairy stems and clusters of linear leaves, to 10 mm long. These leaves often have short recurved points. Flowers yellow with red centre; they occur singly at or near the ends of small side branches. Pod rounded, inflated, to 5 mm long.

Flowering period	Aug. to Oct.
Distribution	In the Sydney area, only found in western suburbs between Windsor and Penrith. Also north coast and tablelands of NSW.
Habitat	Woodland and open forest, in clay or gravelly soils.
Notes	A vulnerable species because of its narrow range. Included on the national rare species list.
Similar species	*D. glaberrima* has hairless branches and clusters of flowers.
Specific sites	Agnes Banks NR, Castlereagh NR, Windsor Downs NR, Scheyville NP.

Family Orchidaceae

Description

Erect ground orchid, mostly leafless as it is parasitic on organic matter in the soil. Flowering stem to 60 cm tall, with numerous showy pink flowers which have purple blotches. Flowers are up to 3 cm across and there may be 20–50 flowers on a single stem.

Flowering period	Dec. to March.
Distribution	Scattered throughout the Sydney region and in many areas of the State; also Qld and Vic.
Habitat	Forest and woodland, in sandy soils.
Notes	This species is saprophytic — it derives its nourishment from organic matter in the soil; hence it has no need for leaves.
Similar species	None in the region.
Specific sites	Oatley Pleasure Grounds, Bents Basin (Nepean River), Maroota–Sackville.

Family Orchidaceae

Description

Small ground orchid with ovoid tubers and two linear leaves arising from the base of the stem. Flowering stem to 50 cm tall, with 2–5 golden yellow flowers which have brown-red markings. Dorsal sepals are yellow, broad and erect like donkey ears; lateral sepals are linear, green and hang down without crossing. Flowers are about 3 cm across.

Flowering period	Sept. to Oct.
Distribution	Scattered along coast north and south of Sydney, extending in some places to adjacent tablelands.
Habitat	Grassy understorey of open forest.
Notes	The specific name 'aurea' is an apt reference to the golden flower.
Similar species	*D. maculata* has flowers with all sections marked with brown and lateral sepals which are usually crossed.
Specific sites	Castlereagh NR, Windsor Downs NR, Brisbane Water NP.

Family Orchidaceae

Description

Small orchid, growing in clumps on rocks, with spreading to hanging stems, and terete succulent leaves, to 10 cm long. Small flowers have cream-yellow sepals and petals, streaked with red, and a white labellum. Flowers are on short stalks in inflorescences of 1 or 2 flowers.

Flowering period	Sept. to Nov.
Distribution	Scattered north and south of Sydney, extending into Blue Mountains. Occurs along coast and tablelands south from Newcastle to Vic and Tas.
Habitat	Sheltered cliff faces and large sandstone boulders in eucalypt forests and rainforests.
Notes	Previously known as *Dendrobium striolatum*. Often abundant, forming dense clumps on rocks.
Similar species	*D. teretifolia* also has long terete leaves, but has inflorescences of 4–15 flowers.
Specific sites	Kellys Falls (upper Hacking River), Bola Creek (Royal NP), Cooks Nose (Barren Grounds).

Family Doryanthaceae

Description

Large plant with clumps of numerous entire leaves, from 1 to 2 m long and 10 cm wide. Deep red flowers are borne in a compact head at the top of a scape which may be 4 m tall. The flowers are surrounded by reddish bracts.

Flowering period	Aug. to Nov.
Distribution	Coastal zone south of Georges River and plateau area north of Hawkesbury River; also near Grafton.
Habitat	Forest and woodland, in sandy soils enriched with clay.
Notes	Flower spike eaten by Aboriginal people; roots also edible after roasting.
Similar species	None in the region.
Specific sites	Waterfall, Heathcote Creek, Calga, Curra Moors (Royal NP).

Family Epacridaceae

Description

Low hanging or prostrate shrub, about 60 cm tall. Leaves narrow, crowded, with acuminate tips and overlapping bases, to 12 cm x 1 cm. Small pink to white flowers are borne along an inflorescence which extends beyond the leaves. Each flower is small (6–8 mm) and hangs like a small bell from the flower stem.

Flowering period	July to Oct.
Distribution	Widespread and common in rocky sandstone areas of Sydney; also Blue Mountains, north coast, south coast and southern tablelands.
Habitat	Moist cliff faces and sheltered wet sandstone rock ledges.
Notes	The generic name of this species means 'dragon leaf'.
Similar species	None in the region.
Specific sites	Bents Basin (Nepean River), Mt Keira Lookout, Maroota–Sackville, Upper Falls (Waterfall).

Family Droseraceae

Description

Small carnivorous plant with erect leaves which are forked and divided into narrow segments and covered with sticky reddish glandular hairs. Flowers white, about 2 cm across and borne on long stalks, to 50 cm tall, well above the leaves.

Flowering period	Nov. to Jan., often following fire.
Distribution	Widespread along coast. Extending to higher Blue Mountains. Scattered along coast and tablelands of the State; also Qld, Vic, SA and Asia.
Habitat	Swampy areas, in peaty soil and full sun.
Notes	Upper surface of leaves have glandular hairs that produce a sticky substance which traps and digests insects.
Similar species	None in the region.
Specific sites	Kurnell, Salvation Creek (West Head), Helensburgh.

Family   Droseraceae

Description

Small carnivorous plant with a rosette of red leaves about 3 cm across. Each leaf is spoon-shaped, 1–2 cm long and covered with sticky glandular hairs. Flowers are either white or pink and borne in groups on one side of a short flower stalk, to 8 cm tall.

Flowering period	Oct. to Feb.
Distribution	Widespread in the Sydney district and Blue Mountains. Occurring throughout coast and tablelands districts of NSW; also Qld, Vic, Tas, NZ and SE Asia.
Habitat	Swampy areas, in sandy soils of low nutrients, in full sun.
Notes	Small red glands on leaves trap and digest insects.
Similar species	*D. pygmaea* is much smaller and has a silver hairy centre to the rosette.
Specific sites	Scheyville NP, Castlereagh NR, Curra Moors (Royal NP).

Family Elaeocarpaceae

Description

Small tree, mostly to 6 m, but sometimes taller, with lance-shaped leaves having regular serrations, to 12 cm x 4 cm. Flowers white (rarely pink), bell-shaped and delicately fringed. They are borne in racemes to 8 cm long. Fruit is round, dark blue, grape-like, to 10 mm diameter.

Flowering period	Nov. to Dec. Berries from June to Oct.
Distribution	Widespread and common in the Sydney district and throughout much of the State; also Qld, Vic and Tas.
Habitat	Sheltered areas of forest, especially on slopes and in gullies, on sandstone, shales and clays.
Notes	Blue berries are a favourite food of currawong; also eaten by native pigeons, regent bowerbirds and crimson rosellas. Pink flowered plants are sold in nurseries.
Similar species	None in the region.
Specific sites	Kurnell, Oatley Park, Carss Park, Devlins Creek (North Epping).

Family Epacridaceae

Description

Erect or straggling shrub, 50–150 cm tall, with spreading, sharp-pointed, heart–shaped leaves, to 12 mm long. Flowers are pendulous red tubes with white lobes, to 2 cm long; they hang in rows from near the tip of the branches. Plants with all white flowers sometimes occur.

Flowering period	Mainly April to Nov.; a few flowers at other times.
Distribution	Widespread and common along the coast in sandy areas. Occurs along north coast and tablelands of NSW; also Qld.
Habitat	Heath, woodland and forest, in sandy soils, often in damp rocky areas.
Notes	The conspicuous flower of this species has long been used as a design in the decorative arts.
Similar species	None in the region.
Specific sites	Kurnell, North Head, Oatley Park, Audley.

Family Epacridaceae

Description

Wiry shrub with erect branches, 30–80 cm tall. Leaves small,
crowded, sharp-pointed, heart-shaped, 3–5 mm long. Flowers
white, with a short tube (4–6 mm long) and 5 spreading lobes, often
pink in bud. Although small and borne singly, the flowers extend
along the upper branches to make a conspicuous show.

Flowering period	June to Nov.
Distribution	Widespread and common in sandy areas of the Sydney district, extending to Blue Mountains and many other areas of the State; also Qld and Vic.
Habitat	Heath and woodland, in sandy soil.
Notes	Easily identified by its erect head of white flowers and its tiny heart-shaped leaves.
Similar species	*E. pulchella* has larger leaves and flowers in autumn.
Specific sites	Kurnell, Castlereagh NR, Curra Moors (Royal NP), Waterfall.

Family Epacridaceae

Description

Erect shrub, to 80 cm tall. Leaves crowded, thick, elliptic, with blunt apex, to 12 mm long. Flowers white to cream bells, to 10 mm long, borne in one-sided racemes at the top of the branches.

Flowering period	July to Jan.
Distribution	Widespread on sandstone areas of Sydney district, extending along coast and tablelands of the State; also Qld, Vic and Tas.
Habitat	Wet heath, in sandy soils and swampy sedgeland.
Notes	The white flower heads of this species may dominate swampy heaths.
Similar species	None in the region.
Specific sites	Maddens Plains, Warrah Sanct. (Patonga), Kurnell, Curra Moors (Royal NP).

Family Epacridaceae

Description

Wiry shrub with erect branches, 30–80 cm tall. Leaves crowded, sharp-pointed, spreading, heart-shaped, 4–6 mm long. Flowers white, 5–8 mm across, with a tube to 5 mm long and 5 spreading lobes. The flowers extend along the upper part of the branches.

Flowering period	March to June.
Distribution	Widespread on sandstone areas of Sydney district, extending to Blue Mountains and coast and tablelands of the State; also Qld.
Habitat	Heath and woodland, in sandy soils.
Notes	This species flowers in autumn and winter, unlike most other white *Epacris* in this area.
Similar species	*E. microphylla* has smaller flowers and leaves.
Specific sites	Bents Basin (Nepean River), Oatley Park, Curra Moors (Royal NP).

Family Rutaceae

Description

Large bushy shrub, to 2 m tall, with narrow leaves, pointed at the tip, to 8 cm x 1 cm. These leaves are alternate, light green and thickish. Flowers are 5-petalled, light pink, with white centres. There are 10 stamens arranged in a pyramid over the ovary.

Flowering period	Aug. to Oct.
Distribution	Widespread in the Sydney district. Occurs along most of NSW coast and central tablelands; also Qld.
Habitat	Forest slopes and heath, in sandy soil.
Notes	The abundant pink, 5-petalled, star-like flowers make this a very attractive plant and it is frequently grown in native gardens.
Similar species	None in the region.
Specific sites	Wedderburn, Sphinx (North Turramurra), Waterfall (Royal NP).

Family Myrtaceae

Description

Tree, to 30 m tall, with spreading canopy and hard, black, corrugated bark extending to the smaller branches. Juvenile leaves are narrow, lanceolate and dull green. Adult leaves are narrow, grey-green, to 12 cm x 1.5 cm. Buds in clusters of 7–11, bud cap shortly conical, followed by white flowers. Fruit cup-shaped, to 6 mm across, with valves at rim level.

Flowering period	Aug. to Dec.
Distribution	Common in west and south-western Sydney; also western slopes and north-western plains of NSW, and Qld.
Habitat	Woodland, in clay soils derived from Wianamatta Shale.
Notes	Often found as a co-dominant tree with *E. moluccana* in Cumberland Plain Woodland.
Similar species	*E. sideroxylon* has larger fruit (to 9 mm across) and 7 flowers per group.
Specific sites	Castlereagh NR, Windsor Downs NR, Mt Annan, Scheyville NP.

Family Myrtaceae

Description

Tree, to 30 m tall, with spreading canopy and hard, black, corrugated bark on the entire tree. Juvenile leaves rounded to ovate in contrast to the broad lanceolate adult leaves which are grey-green, to 18 cm x 5 cm. Buds are in clusters of 7 (sometimes more), with a distinctive elongated pixie-cap. White flowers are followed by cup-shaped fruit, to 10 mm across, with protruding valves.

Flowering period	Nov. to Feb.
Distribution	Common in western Sydney, especially Cumberland Plain between East Hills and Penrith. Scattered along coast, central tablelands and western slopes of NSW; also Qld.
Habitat	Grassy or shrubby open forest, on clay, alluvium or sandy soils.
Notes	This species is the dominant tree in reserves like Castlereagh NR and Windsor Downs NR, often forming pure stands.
Similar species	*E. paniculata* has fruit with valves enclosed, a short conical bud cap and leaves to 3 cm wide.
Specific sites	Castlereagh NR, Windsor Downs NR, Padstow Park, Mitchell Park (Cattai), Carysfield Park (Bass Hill).

121

Family Myrtaceae

Description

Tree, to 15 m tall, spreading or crooked, with smooth white to grey
bark marked with insect 'scribbles'. Juvenile leaves ovate and dull
green in contrast to lanceolate glossy green adult leaves, to 12 cm x
3 cm. Buds in clusters of 11 or more, bud cap shortly conical,
followed by white flowers. Fruit cup-shaped, 6–9 mm across, flat on
top, with valves at rim level.

Flowering period	Mostly Nov. to Aug., but some flowers at other times.
Distribution	Widespread and common in the coastal zone between Royal NP and Wyong; also north coast of NSW.
Habitat	Woodland, on sandy ridges and plateaux.
Notes	Distinctive scribbles on bark caused by the larvae of Scribble Moth.
Similar species	*E. racemosa* has dull adult leaves, smaller fruit and occurs mainly north of Port Jackson. *E. sclerophylla* is a larger tree with smaller fruit and occurs mainly in western Sydney.
Specific sites	Kurnell, West Head, Castlereagh NR, Engadine (Royal NP).

Family Myrtaceae

Description

Large mallee, to 6 m tall, with numerous smooth whitish stems
rising from a lignotuber. Adult leaves green to glaucous, sickle-
shaped, to 18 cm x 3 cm, with a distinctive yellow mid-vein. Buds
in clusters of 11 or more, borne on flattened glaucous flower stalks.
White flowers are followed by large bell-shaped fruit, to 10 mm
diameter, flat on top, with valves enclosed.

Flowering period	July to Dec.
Distribution	Restricted to sandstone areas of Sydney between Gosford and O'Hares Creek (Darkes Forest).
Habitat	Heath and shrubland, often on rocky sites.
Notes	On national rare species list because of its restricted range and scattered and isolated populations.
Similar species	None in the region.
Specific sites	Bantry Bay, Wallaroo Track (Ku-ring-gai Chase), Mt Bass (Royal NP), Waterfall.

Family Myrtaceae

Description

Tree, to 25 m tall, with grey short-fibrous bark on the lower trunk; upper branches are smooth. Juvenile leaves rounded to ovate and dull grey-green in contrast to the sickle-shaped glossy green adult leaves which are up to 14 cm long and 3 cm wide. Buds in clusters of 7, bud caps cone-shaped and followed by white flowers. Fruit cylindrical to urn-shaped, to 6 mm across, with 3–4 valves enclosed.

Flowering period	Very variable. Feb. to April; also June and July.
Distribution	Common in western Sydney and widely distributed in the State; also Qld.
Habitat	Woodland, in soils derived from Wianamatta Shale.
Notes	An important and often dominant component of the threatened Cumberland Plain Woodland.
Similar species	*E. bosistoana* has narrower leaves (to 18 mm wide) and 5–6 valves in fruit.
Specific sites	Cecil Park, Windsor Downs NR, Penrith–Windsor, Werombi–The Oaks, Lansdowne Park.

Family Myrtaceae

Description

Mallee, to 4 m tall, with numerous slender smooth white or green-grey stems rising from a lignotuber. Smaller stems often reddish. Adult leaves glossy green, broad lanceolate, to 10 cm x 2.5 cm. Buds yellow, in clusters of 7; bud cap short, pointed and minutely warty. White flowers are followed by urn-shaped fruit, to 12 mm across, with valves enclosed.

Flowering period	July–Dec.
Distribution	Scattered north of Sydney to Ku-ring-gai Chase NP and common to the south in Royal NP. A few occurrences in eastern suburbs. Extends south to Jervis Bay.
Habitat	Mallee heath, in sandy soils.
Notes	Mallees like this species have large lignotubers from which new growth emerges after fire.
Similar species	*E. obstans* intergrades with *E. stricta* which is also a mallee but with much narrower leaves and smaller buds and fruit. These intergrades occur in Royal NP and flower in December.
Specific sites	North Head, Maroubra, Wattamolla, Curra Moors (Royal NP).

Family Myrtaceae

Description

Tree, to 35 m tall, with spreading canopy and hard black corrugated bark on the entire tree. Juvenile leaves ovate; adult leaves lanceolate, glossy green, paler on undersurface, to 12 cm x 3 cm. Buds in clusters of 7, with a short conical bud cap. White flowers are followed by ovoid, flat-topped fruit, to 8 mm across, with valves enclosed.

Flowering period	May to Aug.
Distribution	Widespread around Sydney; also south coast, north coast, central tablelands and central western slopes of NSW.
Habitat	Moist forest, often with Turpentine, in richer shales, alluvium and volcanic soils.
Notes	The habitat of this species has been heavily cleared for housing, and remnants, such as around Bankstown, are a small part of what was previously an extensive Turpentine–Ironbark forest.
Similar species	*E. fibrosa* has leaves to 5 cm wide, an elongated bud cap and exserted valves in fruit.
Specific sites	Appin, Bankstown area, Reids Flat (Audley), West Head (Ku-ring-gai Chase).

Family Myrtaceae

Description

Tree, to 16 m tall, spreading, often with drooping branches. Bark smooth, grey-white. Leaves sickle-shaped, dull green, to 16 cm x 2.5 cm. Buds in clusters of 7; bud caps short conical and often reddish. Flowers white, followed by cup-shaped fruit, to 9 mm across, with pointed protruding valves.

Flowering period	Nov. to Jan.
Distribution	Western and south-western Sydney, extending from Howes Valley to Hill Top.
Habitat	Woodland, in sandy, shale and alluvial soils, often in poorly drained depressions.
Notes	Often found in association with *Melaleuca decora*.
Similar species	None in the region.
Specific sites	East Hills, Agnes Banks NR, Castlereagh NR, Rickabys Creek (Londonderry).

Family Myrtaceae

Description

Large straight or spreading tree, growing to 40 m or more, with grey to black fibrous bark as a stocking on the lower trunk, but with upper trunk and branches smooth. Juvenile leaves opposite, sessile and paler on undersurface; adult leaves lanceolate, glossy green, to 13 cm x 3 cm. Buds in clusters of 7–15; bud caps conical with a distinct beak. White flowers are followed by cup-shaped fruit, to 12 mm across, with valves enclosed.

Flowering period	Sept. to March.
Distribution	Widespread and common in the Sydney district. Occurs along coast and northern tablelands of NSW; also Qld.
Habitat	Often the dominant tree of coastal forest and protected slopes, in sandy and shale soils.
Notes	One of Australia's most important hardwood trees. Planted in many countries overseas.
Similar species	None in the region.
Specific sites	Oatley, Carss Park, Forest Island (Royal NP), Devlins Creek–Lane Cove River.

Family Myrtaceae

Description

Tree, to 20 m tall, usually with short bole and crooked spreading branches. Bark grey, often black from fire, short-fibrous on trunk and lower branches; smaller branches smooth. Adult leaves lanceolate, dull green, to 12 cm x 2 cm, with a strong peppermint scent when crushed. Buds in clusters of 11–15; bud caps short conical. Flowers white, followed by globose fruit, to 7 mm across, with valves enclosed.

Flowering period	Nov. to Jan.
Distribution	Widespread and common on sandstone areas in the Sydney district, extending to the Blue Mountains. Occurs along coast and southern tablelands of NSW.
Habitat	Woodland and forest, in sandy soil.
Notes	Eucalyptus oil was distilled from this species in colonial days.
Similar species	*E. sieberi* has dark bark and red young branches.
Specific sites	Kurnell, Waterfall, Pennant Hills Park, Oatley Park.

Family Myrtaceae

Description

Tree, to 30 m tall, with smooth bark which is patched grey, white-grey and orange depending on the season as bark is shed. Adult leaves lanceolate, glossy dark green, to 12 cm x 3 cm. Buds distinctly yellow, in clusters of 7; bud caps conical. Flowers white, followed by cup-shaped fruit, to 10 mm across, with protruding valves.

Flowering period	Dec. to March.
Distribution	Widespread and common in the Sydney district. Occurs along NSW coast, tablelands and central western slopes.
Habitat	Open forest, usually on sandstone slopes with localised shale influences or loamy soils.
Notes	Leaves eaten by koalas and blossoms visited by grey-headed fruit-bats.
Similar species	None in the region.
Specific sites	East Hills Park, Bobbin Head, Devlins Creek (Lane Cove NP), Mitchell Park (Cattai).

Family Myrtaceae

Description

Tree, to 25 m tall, with thick spongy fibrous bark on trunk and extending to smaller branches. Adult leaves broad lanceolate, dark green, lighter underneath, to 18 cm x 4 cm. Buds in cluster of 7–11; each bud relatively large, to 20 mm long. Bud caps conical and distinctly beaked. Flowers white, followed by cylindrical fruit, to 12 mm across, with valves to rim level.

Flowering period	April to Sept.
Distribution	Scattered along coast, especially near estuaries. Occurring all along NSW coast; also Qld.
Habitat	Swampy forests or in brackish sandy areas.
Notes	A key species for birds and flying-foxes as it is the only significant winter flowering tree along the coast.
Similar species	*E. botryoides* has bud caps which are short conical; it flowers Jan. to April.
Specific sites	Kurnell, Carss Park, La Perouse, Lower Portland.

Family Myrtaceae

Description

Impressive large straight tree, to 40 m tall, with a smooth white to grey bark. Juvenile leaves ovate, with wavy margins. Adult leaves broad lanceolate, glossy, dark green, paler underneath, to 18 cm x 3 cm. Buds in clusters of 7–11; bud cap conical and sharply pointed. White flowers are followed by bell-shaped fruit, to 7 mm across, with valves slightly protruding.

Flowering period	Jan. to April.
Distribution	North Shore of Sydney, and Gosford to Wyong. Occurs along the north coast and northern tablelands of NSW; also Qld.
Habitat	Tall sheltered forests, especially in clay-shale soils.
Notes	Leaves eaten by koalas; bell miners and other birds forage among higher branches. This species was heavily logged in early 19th century to supply hardwood for ship building and floorboards.
Similar species	Hybrids between *E. saligna* and *E. botryoides* are a common tall tree south of Sydney, especially around Wollongong.
Specific sites	Hornsby Valley, Lane Cove NP, Dalrymple–Hay NR (Pymble).

Family Myrtaceae

Description

Tree, to 30 m tall, usually with a straight trunk and smooth white-grey bark marked with insect 'scribbles'. Adult leaves lanceolate, hard, glossy green, to 12 cm x 4 cm. Buds in clusters of 11 or more; bud caps shortly conical, followed by white flowers. Fruit cup-shaped, 4–6 mm across, flat on top, with valves at rim level.

Flowering period	Dec. to March.
Distribution	Western Sydney, extending to Blue Mountains and Southern Highlands; also south coast and southern tablelands of NSW.
Habitat	Woodland, in sandy soil and Tertiary alluvium.
Notes	Often associated with trees of *Angophora bakeri*.
Similar species	*E. haemastoma* is a smaller tree with larger fruits.
	E. racemosa is also a smaller tree, occurring chiefly north of Port Jackson.
Specific sites	East Hills Park, Agnes Banks NR, Holsworthy, Scheyville NP.

Family Myrtaceae

Description

Tree, to 30 m tall, with spreading canopy and hard black deeply furrowed bark extending to the smaller branches. Adult leaves lanceolate, grey-green, to 12 cm x 1.8 cm. Buds in clusters of 7; bud cap short conical. Flowers white or pink, followed by globose to urn-shaped fruit, to 9 mm across, with valves enclosed.

Flowering period	April to Oct.
Distribution	Scattered throughout western Sydney and in many western areas of the State; also Qld and Vic.
Habitat	Woodland, in sandy soil and alluvium.
Notes	Name derived from Greek 'sideros' (iron) and 'xylon' (wood), a reference to the hard red timber.
Similar species	*E. crebra* has smaller fruit (to 6 mm across) and 7–11 flowers per group. *E. fibrosa* has long 'pixie cap' bud caps.
Specific sites	Moorebank, Windsor Downs NR, Shanes Park, Castlereagh NR.

Eucalyptus sieberi   Black Ash, Silvertop Ash

Family Myrtaceae

Description

Spreading tree, to 20 m tall, with grey to black fibrous bark extending to larger branches, but upper branchlets smooth. New growth distinctly red. Adult leaves lanceolate, glossy green, shiny, to 15 cm x 2.5 cm. Buds in clusters of 7–15; bud cap shortly conical, followed by masses of small white flowers. Fruit is barrel-shaped to conical, to 9 mm across, flat on top, with valves enclosed.

Flowering period	Sept. to Dec.
Distribution	Common on sandstone areas north and south of Sydney, extending to Blue Mountains and Southern Highlands. Occurs on south coast and southern tablelands of NSW; also Vic and Tas.
Habitat	Open forest, on exposed sandy ridges and upper slopes.
Notes	The most common tree beside the Princes Highway between Waterfall and Wollongong. Dwarfed and mallee forms are found on Curra Moors, Royal NP.
Similar species	*E. piperita* also has fibrous bark, but is without the red young branchlets.
Specific sites	Waterfall, Maddens Plains, Curra Moors Track (Royal NP).

Family Moraceae

Description

Small tree, to 10 m tall, with spreading hairy branches. Leaves oblong to elliptic, to 10 cm x 5 cm, with upper surface rough like sandpaper. Figs densely hairy, to 2 cm long, green when immature and purple-black when ripe. The tiny flowers within the fig fruit are pollinated by wasps.

Flowering period	Fruits ripe from Jan. to June.
Distribution	Scattered in Sydney district, common in Illawarra. Occurring throughout coast, tablelands and western slopes of the State; also Qld, Vic and NT.
Habitat	Rainforest, sheltered creek banks and shady rocky areas.
Notes	Fruits edible after removal of hairs. Leaves used by Aboriginal people for sanding of wooden weapons.
Similar species	None in the region.
Specific sites	Lane Cove River, Bola Creek (Royal NP), Mitchell Park (Cattai).

Family Moraceae

Description

Variable plant, often a stunted shrub growing from rock crevices, but it may grow into a large spreading tree. Leaves elliptic, dark green, hairless above, rusty hairy below, to 10 cm x 6 cm. Fig globose, to 2 cm long, green–yellow when immature, red when ripe and marked with small warts. Stalk on fruit is short, 2–5 mm long. The tiny flowers within the fig fruit are pollinated by wasps.

Flowering period	Fruits ripe from Feb. to July.
Distribution	Widespread around Sydney, extending to Blue Mountains and Southern Highlands. Occurring throughout coast, tablelands and western slopes of the State; also Qld.
Habitat	Sheltered cliffs, rocky gullies, rainforest margins and protected areas of open forest.
Notes	This fig germinates and spends the early part of its life on rocks. Fruits are eaten by flying-foxes, currawongs and other birds.
Similar species	*F. macrophylla* is a rainforest species from Illawarra and a common tree in Sydney parks. It has larger leaves and fruit stalks to 15 mm long.
Specific sites	Bobbin Head, Razorback Mt, Oatley Park, Wattamolla.

Family Euphorbiaceae

Description

Medium tree, to 10 m tall, with alternate, glossy green, elliptic leaves, to 8 cm x 3.5 cm. Flowers minute, only 3 mm long, greenish yellow and borne in leaf axils. The fruit capsule is the most distinctive feature, as it is shaped like a pumpkin or old fashioned cheese, to 2 cm across, and divided into a number of cells. These ripen and split to release seeds which are covered with a red aril (special seed covering).

Flowering period	Aug. to Dec. Fruit ripe Dec. to April.
Distribution	Widespread in coastal areas, especially along bays and estuaries. Occurring all along NSW coast; also Qld, NT and WA.
Habitat	Sheltered slopes, coastal dunes and along creek banks, in both sandy and clay-shale soils.
Notes	Seeds eaten by many bird species. Some old trees remain as remnants along suburban streets and in parks.
Similar species	None in the region.
Specific sites	Oatley, Carss Park, Bobbin Head, Palm Jungle (Royal NP).

Glycine clandestina

Love Creeper

Family Fabaceae

Description

A twining plant with slender stems covered in soft hairs. Leaves divided into narrow leaflets which are variable in size but mostly to 5 cm x 0.5 cm. The 3 leaflets are on stalks of the same length. Delicate pink to rose-purple pea flowers are in clusters in the upper leaf axils, followed by straight pods, about 4 cm long.

Flowering period	Chiefly Aug. to Dec., but some flowers at other times.
Distribution	Widespread and common in the Sydney district and throughout much of the State; also Qld, Vic, Tas and SA.
Habitat	Grassland, woodland and moist forest, especially on protected hillsides.
Notes	A complex and varied species with many different forms.
Similar species	*G. tabacina* has the central leaflet on a stalk longer than the two side leaflets; it grows mainly in clay soils.
Specific sites	Castlereagh NR, Oatley Park, Lansdowne Park.

Family Fabaceae

Description

Low decumbent shrub, to 30 cm tall, with slender branches, densely warty, from which rise small leaves divided into 5–7 narrow leaflets. Each leaflet is about 10 mm long. Flower is a bright yellow pea. A few flowers are borne in terminal heads on flower stalks to 10 mm long. Fruit is a globular inflated pod, to 10 mm long.

Flowering period	Aug. to Nov.
Distribution	Widespread on sandstone areas of the Sydney district, extending to the Blue Mountains. Occurs all along coast and tablelands of NSW; also Vic.
Habitat	Heath and woodland, in sandy soil.
Notes	Yellow flowers near the ground are probably adapted for the dispersal of seed by ants.
Similar species	*G. pinnatum* has 15–25 leaflets.
Specific sites	Lucas Heights, Castlereagh NR, Sphinx (North Turramurra), Engadine (Royal NP).

Family Fabaceae

Description

Erect shrub, to 1 m tall, with smooth hairless stems and leaves divided into 3. Each leaflet is narrow, up to 30 mm long but only 1 mm wide. Flowers are large yellow peas, to 25 mm long, borne near the ends of the branches on a short stalk. The keel of the flower is without the conspicuous white hairs of *G. latifolium*. Fruit is a globular inflated pod, to 15 mm long.

Flowering period	Aug. to Nov.
Distribution	Widespread in the Sydney district and lower Blue Mountains. Restricted to coastal zones and central tablelands of NSW.
Habitat	Open forest, woodland and heath, usually on sandstone soils.
Notes	Despite the specific name 'grandiflorum', the flowers of this species are no more 'grand' than those of *G. latifolium*.
Similar species	*G. latifolium* has conspicuous white hairs on the keel of its flower.
Specific sites	Lane Cove NP, Kurnell, Mitchell Park, Curra Moors (Royal NP).

Family Goodeniaceae

Description

Ground-hugging small plant with a basal rosette of leaves and similar leaves spread along the delicate stems. Leaves circular to elliptic, variable in size, to 10 mm long, and with margins either lobed or entire. Yellow flowers fan-shaped, to 13 mm long, borne on upright thin stalks.

Flowering period	Sept. to April.
Distribution	Widespread in the Sydney district; also tablelands and western slopes of NSW, Vic and Qld.
Habitat	Open forest, woodland and grassland.
Notes	The name 'hederacea' is a reference to the ivy-like leaves. *Hedera* is the introduced ivy.
Similar species	None in the region.
Specific sites	Windsor Downs NR, Lansdowne Park, Oatley Park, Mt Annan.

Family Goodeniaceae

Description

Variable shrub, sometimes prostrate, but mostly erect, to 1.5 m tall, with a glossy varnished appearance. Leaves shiny and sticky, ovate, with toothed margins, to 6 cm x 3 cm. Flowers yellow, to 16 mm long, fan-shaped and borne in inflorescences shorter than the leaves.

Flowering period	Sept. to Dec.; some flowers at other times.
Distribution	Widespread in the Sydney district and throughout most of the State; also Qld, Vic, SA and Tas.
Habitat	Creek banks and moist open forest, usually in damp shaded places on richer clay and volcanic soils.
Notes	Leaves of this species are often quite sticky from varnish-like resin.
Similar species	None in the region.
Specific sites	West Head (Pittwater), Bents Basin (Nepean River), Bola Creek (Royal NP).

Family Goodeniaceae

Description

Small herbaceous plant, about 40 cm tall, with leaves mostly at the base of the stem, and only a few scattered along the stem. Leaves narrow, entire, thick, glossy, to 15 cm long. Flowers yellow, to 15 mm long, fan-shaped, without a stalk and borne along the upright stem. The back of each flower has white cotton and yellow star-like hairs.

Flowering period	July to Dec.
Distribution	Restricted in the Sydney district to coastal areas between Broken Bay and Waterfall. Also recorded from north coast, south coast, southern tablelands and Qld.
Habitat	Swampy areas and moist sandy scrub.
Notes	The tiny stellate (star-like) hairs on the outside of the flowers of this species are a characteristic feature.
Similar species	*G. bellidifolia* has simple, not stellate, hairs on the flowers. *G. dimorpha* has stalked flowers.
Specific sites	La Perouse, Kurnell, Bundeena (Royal NP).

Family Proteaceae

Description

Erect shrub, to 2 m tall, with a number of forms. Stem hairy brown.
Leaves ovate to elliptic, to 2 cm long, with lower surfaces silky hairy.
Flowers terminal, grey in appearance because of woolly hairs. Style
with white-grey hairs, ending in a horn-like appendage, 1–4 mm
long. Fruit a hairy, boat-shaped follicle.

Flowering period	July to Dec.
Distribution	Widespread in sandstone areas around Sydney. Subspecies extending to Blue Mountains and Southern Highlands.
Habitat	Woodland and heath, in sandy soil.
Notes	Clusters of grey flowers at the ends of erect stems make this an easy plant to identify.
Similar species	Ssp. *sphacelata* has smaller flowers, no style appendage and is the common grey grevillea in Royal NP. Ssp. *phylicoides*, with smaller flowers, occurs in the Blue Mountains.
Specific sites	Bobbin Head, Devlins Creek (North Epping), Windsor Downs NR, Flat Rock Creek (Royal NP).

Family Proteaceae

Description

Large spreading shrub, to 4 m tall, with slender, somewhat drooping branchlets. Leaves long, narrow, silky hairy underneath, to 10 cm long and 1–3 mm wide. Flowers white, silky hairy, sometimes pink in bud. Fruit is a thin-walled boat-shaped follicle.

Flowering period	July to Oct.
Distribution	Coastal, chiefly north of Sydney where it is very common in some patches of bushland. Widespread in eastern part of NSW; also Qld, Vic and SA.
Habitat	Open forest, often on sheltered slopes and in gullies.
Notes	This species has a number of forms. The southern sandstone form (e.g. in Budderoo NP) is a smaller plant, with shorter elliptic leaves which are pungent. Other forms occur on the north coast of NSW and higher Blue Mountains.
Similar species	None in the region.
Specific sites	Bobbin Head, Middle Head, Devlins Creek (North Epping).

Family Proteaceae

Description

Large spreading shrub, to 5 m tall, with angular silky branches.
Leaves long, to 20 cm, coarsely toothed, with the undersurface
covered in silky hairs. Flowers red, and borne in toothbrush-like
inflorescences from leaf axils near the ends of smaller branches.
Fruit is a hairy boat-shaped follicle, with reddish stripes.

Flowering period July to Nov.

Distribution   Scattered but infrequent south of Sydney to Appin
                 and Cataract River.

Habitat   Along or near creeks, in sandy soil.

Notes   Old plants which have escaped bushfire may be
                 4–5 m tall and very spreading.

Similar species *G. aspleniifolia* has densely downy branches; it occurs
                 in Blue Mountains and Southern Highlands.

Specific sites   Heathcote Creek, upper Georges River, O'Hares
                 Creek (Darkes Forest).

Family Proteaceae

Description

Spreading or low shrub, to 1.5 m tall, with ovate to elliptic leaves, dark green above, silky grey below, with a pointed tip, to 25 mm x 12 mm. Flowers mostly green, with a red style and distinctly hairy. Flowers in groups of 6 or more at the end of short branchlets. Fruit is a hairy thin-walled follicle.

Flowering period	April to Oct.
Distribution	Widespread in the Sydney district. Scattered along south coast and central tablelands of NSW.
Habitat	Open forest and woodland, in both sandy and clay soils.
Notes	Leaf shape is very variable in this species, with a noticeable difference between plants growing in sand and in clay.
Similar species	None in the region.
Specific sites	Castlereagh NR, Windsor Downs NR, Oatley Park, Flat Rock Creek (Royal NP).

Family Proteaceae

Description

Shrub, with slender spreading stems, to 2 m tall. Leaves narrow elliptic, silky underneath, with a sharp pointed tip, sometimes in whorls of 3, to 3 cm long and 5–8 mm wide. Flowers a cluster of pink tubes (sometimes mauve or white) and pink–white styles, about 15 mm long. Buds, flowers and flower stalks all have soft silky hairs. Fruit is a hairless boat-shaped follicle.

Flowering period	Mainly July to Dec., with a few flowers at other times.
Distribution	Widespread and common on sandstone areas of Sydney district, extending to Blue Mountains.
Habitat	Open forest and woodland, in sandy soil.
Notes	The flowers of this species are very variable in colour. They range from white (as in Oatley Park) to deep mauve (in lower Blue Mountains).
Similar species	None in the region.
Specific sites	Kurnell, Mt Colah, Engadine (Royal NP).

Family Proteaceae

Description

Spreading shrub, mostly 1–2 m tall, with silky hairy young branches. Leaves narrow, elliptic to short obovate, silky underneath, with a pointed tip, to 3 cm long and 5–10 mm wide. Deep red flowers in hanging clusters; styles to 25 mm long. Buds, flowers and flower stalks all have soft silky hairs. Fruit is a hairless thin-walled follicle.

Flowering period	June to Sept.
Distribution	Restricted to sandstone areas north of Sydney.
Habitat	Open forest, woodland and heath, in sandy soil.
Notes	This is the common red spider flower of the northern suburbs.
Similar species	*G. oleoides* is the common erect red-flowered grevillea south of Sydney and in lower Blue Mountains.
Specific sites	North Head, Sphinx (North Turramurra), Warrah Sanct. (Patonga), Pennant Hills Park.

Family Proteaceae

Description

Compact upright shrub, to 2 m tall, with branches and young leaves covered with dense longish hairs. Leaves needle-like, to 6 cm long. Flowers yellowish-white, borne along the stems within the plant. Flower followed by a large woody globose fruit, to 25 mm wide, which is distinctly beaked and very warty.

Flowering period	June to Sept.
Distribution	Widespread and endemic in coastal sandstone zone north and south of Sydney.
Habitat	Woodland, scrub and heath, in sandy soil.
Notes	A distinctive shrub because of its tightly packed, prickly and hairy appearance.
Similar species	None in the region.
Specific sites	Kurnell, Pearl Beach, Curra Moors (Royal NP).

Family Proteaceae

Description

Upright shrub, to 2 m tall, with crowded needle-like leaves, to 4 cm long, each with a distinct mucro. Flowers white, in small clusters, which often extend along the upper stems. Fruit is large, globose, to 30 mm wide, covered with rough protuberances but without a distinct beak.

Flowering period	May to Aug.
Distribution	Widespread along coast north and south of Sydney, extending to the Blue Mountains.
Habitat	Woodland and scrub, in sandy soil.
Notes	The large woody fruits are held on the plant unopened until fire kills the parent plant; then the seeds are released. A yellow flowered form occurs in the Blue Mountains.
Similar species	*H. sericea* has smaller woody fruit, distinctly beaked.
Specific sites	Warrah Sanct. (Patonga), Maroota–Sackville, Waterfall–Uloola Falls.

Family Proteaceae

Description

Large shrub or small tree, to 5 m tall, with flat, lance-shaped leaves, to 10 cm long. Only the mid-vein of the leaf is distinct, smaller veins are obscure. Flowers white, in small clusters from the leaf axils along the ends of the branches. Fruit is woody, globose, to 20 mm wide, covered with raised blunt warts and with a small beak.

Flowering period	Sept. to Nov.
Distribution	Widespread in Sydney district, extending to Blue Mountains. Occurs all along NSW coast and northern tablelands.
Habitat	Moist forest, protected gullies and along creeks.
Notes	One of only two *Hakea* species in the Sydney area which do not have needle-like leaves.
Similar species	*H. dactyloides* also has flat leaves, but they have 3 or more prominent longitudinal veins.
Specific sites	Heathcote Creek, Maroota–Sackville, Curra Moors Track (Royal NP).

Family Proteaceae

Description

Spreading shrub, to 3 m tall. Leaves needle-like, to 5 cm long, with a rigid sharp tip. These leaves tend to be at right angles to the stem. Flowers white, in small clusters from the leaf axils along the ends of the branches. Fruit is woody, globose to ovoid, to 25 mm wide, moderately warty, with a short beak.

Flowering period	July to Sept.
Distribution	Widespread on sandstone areas of Sydney district and along most of coast and tablelands of NSW; also Vic, SA and Tas.
Habitat	Open forest, scrub and heath, in sandy and clay soils.
Notes	A common and abundant species.
Similar species	*H. propinqua* has larger woody fruit without a distinct beak.
Specific sites	Kurnell, Castlereagh NR, Sphinx (North Turramurra), Engadine (Royal NP)

Family Proteaceae

Description

Large shrub, to 3 m tall, with spreading rigid branches and crowded needle-like leaves, to 5 cm long, with a sharp tip. Flowers white, covered in short white hairs and borne in small but abundant clusters from the leaf axils. Fruit is a woody follicle, long and narrow like a bird's beak or dagger.

Flowering period	Nov. to March.
Distribution	Widespread in the Sydney district and along the coast and tablelands of the State; also Vic and Tas.
Habitat	Scrub and heath, especially in swampy sites and damp sandy depressions.
Notes	This species is unusual for a *Hakea* as it does not have rounded fruit and it begins flowering in summer. It may dominate swampy areas.
Similar species	There are other needle-like *Hakea*, but this is the only one in the area with narrow fruit capsules.
Specific sites	Kurnell, Maddens Plains, Goarra Rill (Engadine), Sphinx (North Turramurra).

Family Fabaceae

Description

Twining plant with long hairless climbing stems. Leaves spear-shaped, strongly veined, about 8 cm long and 3.5 cm wide. Flowers are purple peas, marked with a yellow centre, and borne in groups of 20 or more in conspicuous racemes. These are followed by oblong pods, to 4 cm long.

Flowering period	July to Oct.
Distribution	Widespread and common in the Sydney district and throughout much of the State; also Qld, Vic, SA and WA.
Habitat	Open forest, woodland and coastal scrub, usually twining over understorey plants.
Notes	Often cultivated. A bushy upright form of this species occurs in clay soils in the western suburbs.
Similar species	None in the region.
Specific sites	Kurnell, Oatley Park, Castlereagh NR, Devlins Creek (North Epping).

Family Asteraceae

Description

Upright shrub, to 1.5 m tall, with woolly white branches. Leaves large, broadly lanceolate, green above and woolly white underneath, to 10 cm x 3 cm. Flower heads to 3 cm diameter, with white bracts and yellow central flowers. Flower heads are clustered together in showy terminal groups of 4–8.

Flowering period	Aug. to Oct.
Distribution	Scattered along coast and adjacent plateaux. Widespread along coast and tablelands of NSW; also Qld and Vic.
Habitat	Eucalypt forest and rainforest margins, especially on hillsides in richer soils.
Notes	The name 'elatum' (from Latin 'elatus' = tall, exalted) is apt for this large conspicuous daisy.
Similar species	None in the region.
Specific sites	Kurnell, Hornsby, Bola Creek (Royal NP).

Family Asteraceae

Description

Small perennial herb, to 30 cm, with woolly ascending stems. Leaves narrow, to 6 cm long at the base of the stems, smaller and fewer on the stems. Leaves woolly, with undersurface paler than above. Flower heads yellow, terminal, solitary, 2–3 cm across. Flower bracts are papery, bright yellow, sometimes tinged with brown.

Flowering period	Oct. to July.
Distribution	Scattered throughout the Sydney district, mainly away from sandstone areas. Widely distributed in the State; also Vic, SA and Tas.
Habitat	Sheltered situations in open forest and grassland, especially in fertile soils of clay and shale.
Notes	New growth is from a woody rootstock after fire.
Similar species	*H. rutidolepis* has decumbent much-branched stems and smaller flower heads.
Specific sites	Castlereagh NR, Windsor Downs NR, Lane Cove NP.

Family Lamiaceae

Description

Slender shrub, to 1.5 m tall, with narrow, almost terete leaves, in whorls of 3, to 15 mm long. Flowers blue to mauve, with 3 spreading lower lobes longer than 2 upper lobes. Calyx 5-lobed; there are 4 stamens. Flowers are borne singly in axils of upper leaves.

Flowering period	June to Feb.
Distribution	Widespread on sandstone areas of Sydney district, extending to Blue Mountains.
Habitat	Woodland and heath, in sandy soil.
Notes	Sometimes mistaken for a mint bush (*Prostanthera*), a genus which has a 2-lobed calyx.
Similar species	None in the region.
Specific sites	West Head, Kurnell, Curra Moors (Royal NP).

Family Dilleniaceae

Description

Twining plant with stems about 2m long, often found hanging over lower shrubs. Leaves ovate, glossy green above, lighter underneath, margins toothed, to 7 cm x 3 cm. Flowers large and yellow, with 5 petals and over 30 stamens; they are borne either from leaf axils or terminal on short stalks.

Flowering period	Aug. to Nov.
Distribution	Widespread in a variety of soil types along the coastal zone; also Blue Mountains and Southern Highlands. Extending along the coast and tablelands from Qld to Vic.
Habitat	Sheltered areas of open forest and scrub, often on the edge of rainforest.
Notes	The species name 'dentata' is from the Latin 'dentatus' (toothed), a reference to its leaves.
Similar species	None in the region.
Specific sites	Kurnell, Devlins Creek (North Turramurra), Curra Moors Track (Royal NP).

Family Dilleniaceae

Description

Small shrub, to 40 cm tall, with crowded, clustered, narrow leaves, to 6 mm long. Yellow 5-petalled flowers have 8–12 stamens surrounding 3 hairless carpels. Flowers are without stalks and are borne along the stems.

Flowering period	July to Dec.
Distribution	Widespread in sandy areas of Sydney district and in coastal and tablelands divisions of NSW; also Qld.
Habitat	Open forest and heath, in sandy soil.
Notes	The species name 'fasciculata' is from the Latin 'fascis' (bundle), a reference to its leaves, and from the same word origin as Fascist, whose symbol was a bundle of rods with an axe in the centre.
Similar species	*H. cistiflora* has 2 hairless carpels and 6 stamens on one side of the carpels.
Specific sites	Agnes Banks NR, La Perouse, North Head.

Family Dilleniaceae

Description

Small erect shrub, to 60 cm tall, with distinctive short, hairless,
spoon-shaped leaves, indented at the apex, with a tapering base, to
12 mm long. Yellow flowers have 10–12 stamens surrounding a
solitary hairless carpel. Flowers are without stalks and borne at the
ends of short shoots.

Flowering period	Aug. to Dec.
Distribution	Scattered throughout sandy areas of Sydney. Also Blue Mountains, south coast, tablelands and western slopes of NSW.
Habitat	Open forest and woodland, in sandy soil with shrubby understorey.
Notes	The species name 'monogyna' is a reference to the single carpel (ovary), a feature of this plant.
Similar species	*H. circumdans* has 3 carpels and 15–30 stamens all around the carpels.
Specific sites	Wattamolla, O'Hares Creek (Darkes Forest), Maroota–Sackville.

Family Dilleniaceae

Description

Erect shrub, to 1 m tall, with shiny hairless reddish stems and glossy lance-shaped leaves, to 2 cm long, which have a tapering base and pointed apex. Yellow flowers have about 11 stamens on one side of 2 silky carpels. Sepals are hairless. Flowers are without stalks and borne either terminally or along stems.

Flowering period	Oct. to Nov.
Distribution	Restricted to sandstone areas of coastal Sydney, where it is uncommon.
Habitat	Open forest, on sheltered slopes, often near creeks and saltwater estuaries.
Notes	The name 'nitida' is from the Latin 'nitere' (to shine), a reference to the glossy leaves of this species. It is included on the national rare species list.
Similar species	*H. bracteata* has densely silky sepals.
Specific sites	Middle Harbour Creek, Lane Cove NP, Oatley Park, Toonoom Falls (Royal NP).

Family Dilleniaceae

Description

Trailing plant, with stems to 5 m long, spreading over the ground or on low vegetation. Leaves obovate, entire, with pointed apex and stem-clasping base, to 7 cm x 2.5 cm. Flowers are large, to 5 cm across, yellow, with 5 petals and over 30 conspicuous stamens. Fruit a follicle, to 4 cm across, splitting at the top to expose seed covered by orange-red aril.

Flowering period	April to Nov.
Distribution	Coastal zone of Sydney district. Extending from south coast of NSW to Qld.
Habitat	Coastal sand dunes, scrub near sea and rainforest margins, in both sandy soils and richer Narrabeen Shales.
Notes	Plants near the sea tend to be more hairy and have spoon-shaped leaves.
Similar species	None in the region.
Specific sites	Kurnell, Oatley Park, Barrenjoey, Bola Creek (Royal NP).

Family Fabaceae

Description

Small erect shrub, to 50 cm tall, with hairy branches and narrow alternate leaves, to 5 cm long and 2–4 mm wide. The upper surface of the leaf is strongly veined and hairless. Flowers light mauve, with darker purple and yellow centres, borne on short stalks. Calyx covered with long grey hairs. Pod globular, inflated, about 8 mm long.

Flowering period	July to Aug.
Distribution	Widespread in the Sydney district and throughout much of the State; also Qld, Vic, SA and Tas.
Habitat	Open forest and heath, in a variety of soils.
Notes	Despite its small size, this species is noticeable as it bears its flowers in winter.
Similar species	None in the region.
Specific sites	Castlereagh NR, Oatley Park, Engadine (Royal NP).

165

Family Fabaceae

Description

Slender spreading shrub, to 2 m tall, with leaves 7–10 cm long, consisting of about 15 oblong leaflets, each about 15 mm long. Numerous pink to mauve flowers are borne along an inflorescence which is as long or longer than the leaves. Fruit is a narrow cylindrical pod, about 3 cm long.

Flowering period	Aug. to Oct.
Distribution	Scattered in the Sydney district; extending to Blue Mountains and Southern Highlands. Occurs throughout most of NSW and all States, except NT.
Habitat	Woodland and forest, often on rocky slopes or on richer clay and shale soils.
Notes	A very large genus world-wide, with about 700 species. Only one species occurs in the Sydney district.
Similar species	None in the region.
Specific sites	Lane Cove NP, Scheyville NP, Garie Beach (Royal NP).

Family Proteaceae

Description

Erect shrub, to 1.5 m tall, with leaves divided into numerous
flattened segments, to 4 mm wide. Yellow flowers are borne in
terminal globose cones, about 25 mm across. These are followed by
fruiting cones resembling drumsticks, globose and up to 16 mm
wide.

Flowering period	Sept. to Nov.
Distribution	Widespread on sandstone areas of the Sydney district, and along most of the coast and tablelands of NSW; also Qld.
Habitat	Open forest, woodland and heath, in sandy soil.
Notes	The botanical name of this species is aptly descriptive. 'Iso' (equal) and 'pogon' (beard) are references to the hairs on the fruit; 'anemoni', 'folius' means 'leaves like those of anemone'.
Similar species	*I. anethifolius* has narrower leaves.
Specific sites	Castlereagh NR, Windsor Downs NR, Waterfall (Royal NP).

Family Proteaceae

Description

Handsome erect shrub, to 2 m tall, with leaves divided into numerous terete segments, which are acute but not pungent pointed. Yellow flowers are borne in terminal globose cones, about 25 mm across. These are followed by fruiting cones resembling drumsticks, globose and up to 25 mm wide.

Flowering period Sept. to Dec.

Distribution	Widespread on sandstone areas of the Sydney district, extending to Blue Mountains, south coast and southern tablelands of NSW.
Habitat	Open forest, woodland and heath, in sandy soil.
Notes	New foliage is a conspicuous tan colour, adding to the attractive appearance of this shrub.
Similar species	*I. anemonifolius* has leaves with flat segments.
Specific sites	Kurnell, Pennant Hills Park, Curra Moors (Royal NP).

Family Fabaceae

Description

Erect shrub, to 3 m tall, with angular leafless branches, greyish in appearance, sometimes with drooping branchlets. Yellow pea flowers are borne in small clusters on the upper part of the branches and are followed by oblong hairy pods, to 12 mm long.

Flowering period	Oct. to Nov.
Distribution	Scattered and localised in the Sydney district and Blue Mountains. Also occurs in many other areas of the State and Qld.
Habitat	Grassy woodland, usually on clay or gravelly soils.
Notes	A conspicuous plant because of its numerous yellow flowers on leafless branches.
Similar species	None in the region.
Specific sites	Moorebank, Scheyville NP, Castlereagh NR, Windsor Downs NR.

Family Fabaceae

Description

Twining plant, with rusty-hairy stems usually draped over low
vegetation. Leaves divided into 3, with each leaflet broad ovate, to
10 cm long. Flowers large, to 4 cm long, dark red, backed by a rust-
coloured hairy calyx and followed by a pod which is 5–10 cm long
and also rust-coloured and hairy.

Flowering period July to Nov.

Distribution Widespread and common along the coast and in Blue
Mountains. Occurs all along coast and tablelands of
NSW; also Qld and Vic.

Habitat Sheltered forest, woodland and coastal scrub, usually
twining over understorey plants.

Notes The rich red pendulous flowers of this species are a
conspicuous feature of the understorey in sandstone
bushland.

Similar species *K. prostrata* is prostrate in habit, with smaller rounded
leaflets.

Specific sites Kurnell, Rookwood Cemetery, Devlins Creek
(North Epping), Curra Moors Track (Royal NP).

Family Myrtaceae

Description

Large spreading shrub, to 3 m tall, with small linear crowded leaves, to 10 mm long. Flowers white, with numerous conspicuous stamens, and crowded along the upper stems. Fruit is a cup–shaped capsule, about 3 mm long.

Flowering period	Late Oct. to Dec.
Distribution	Widespread and common along coast and nearby plateaux. Occurs along coast and tablelands south of Sydney; also Vic and Tas.
Habitat	Woodland, scrub and heath, usually in sandy soil.
Notes	A coloniser of bare and disturbed sites. Prolific white flowers are an important nectar source for native insects.
Similar species	None in the region.
Specific sites	Kurnell, Oatley Park, Bobbin Head, Castlereagh NR.

Family Myrtaceae

Description

Small erect shrub, mostly less than 1 m tall, with crowded obovate leaves, to 9 mm long, which have 3 distinct longitudinal veins and recurved apex. Flowers purple-pink, with numerous stamens and in terminal heads.

Flowering period	Sept. to Nov.
Distribution	Widespread and common along the coast and adjacent ranges. Occurs along most of NSW coast, central tablelands and southern tablelands.
Habitat	Heath and woodland, in shallow sandy soil.
Notes	A white-flowered form occurs at Barren Grounds NR, Budderoo NP and other areas south of Sydney.
Similar species	*K. parvifolia* also has pink flower heads, but has smaller leaves with only the mid-vein visible.
Specific sites	Curracurrong (Royal NP), Waterfall–Uloola Falls, Agnes Banks NR, North Head.

Lambertia formosa **Honey Flower, Mountain Devil**

Family Proteaceae

Description

Spreading shrub, to 2 m tall, with narrow rigid pungent leaves, mostly in whorls of 3, to 6 cm long. Tubular red flowers united into a cluster of 7, surrounded by large bracts. Flower tubes up to 4 cm long, with a thin style projecting 10–15 mm beyond the tube. Fruit a woody follicle with 2 valves and a beak and horn on each valve, resembling the head of a 'mountain devil'.

Flowering period	Sept. to May.
Distribution	Widespread on sandstone areas in the Sydney district; also Blue Mountains, north coast, south coast and southern tablelands of the State.
Habitat	Open forest, woodland and heath, in sandy soil.
Notes	Flowers produce abundant nectar for honeyeaters. Fruit once used as heads for 'mountain devil' souvenirs.
Similar species	None in the region.
Specific sites	Oatley Park, Waterfall–Uloola Falls, Bents Basin (Nepean River).

Family Sterculiaceae

Description

Erect shrub, to 1 m tall. Young branches, lower surfaces of leaves and
calyx covered with rust-coloured hairs. Leaves narrow, oblong,
hairless above, to 8 cm x 1 cm. Flowers in dense clusters. Petals
minute but 5 segments of calyx conspicuous, to 8 mm long, deep
rust-brown outside, hairy and white inside.

Flowering period	Aug. to Nov.
Distribution	Widespread in the Sydney district, extending to adjacent tablelands and Blue Mountains. Occurs along most of NSW coast and Vic.
Habitat	Forest and woodland, in sandy soil.
Notes	The genus name is descriptive: 'lasios' (hairy); 'petalum' (petal), a reference to the most distinctive feature of this genus.
Similar species	Ssp. *cordatum* has broad, heart-shaped leaves. *L. rufum* has reddish flowers.
Specific sites	Sphinx (North Turramurra), Curra Moors (Royal NP), Oatley Park, Bents Basin (Nepean River).

Family Rutaceae

Description

Large shrub or small tree, to 5 m tall. Leaves alternate, narrow, to 6 cm x 0.5 cm, white and hairy underneath and with a blunt or V-shaped apex; leaf margins have small fine teeth and are curled under. Flowers yellow, with 5 petals and 10 prominent stamens. They are borne abundantly in clusters of about 10 from the leaf axils on stalks shorter than the leaves.

Flowering period	Aug. to Oct.
Distribution	Scattered north and south of Sydney, extending to lower Blue Mountains and Southern Highlands; also north coast and northern tablelands of NSW.
Habitat	Open forest, usually in gullies, in sandy soil or among sandstone rocks.
Notes	Previously known as *Phebalium dentatum*, this attractive plant is often found along creek banks where it is very conspicuous when in flower,
Similar species	None in the region.
Specific sites	Girrakool, Devlins Creek (North Epping), O'Hares Creek (Darkes Forest), Heathcote Creek.

Family Santalaceae

Description

Large shrub, to 3 m tall, with slender green striate branches, apparently leafless as minute scale-like leaves are deciduous. Flowers greenish-yellow, very small and borne in spikes up to 3 cm long. These are followed by round, green, fleshy fruits, to 6 mm diam.

Flowering period	Feb. to April. Fruits ripe May to Aug.
Distribution	Widespread on coastal sandstone areas in the Sydney district, extending to the Blue Mountains. Occurs along most of NSW coast and tablelands; also Qld and Vic.
Habitat	Open forest, in sandy soil.
Notes	A semi-parasitic plant on the roots of nearby plants. Ripe fruits edible and thirst quenching.
Similar species	None in the region.
Specific sites	Waterfall, Oatley Park, Curra Moors (Royal NP).

Family Myrtaceae

Description

Low rigid divaricate and frequently prostrate shrub, with flaky bark on old wood. Leaves clustered, narrow, concave, pungent pointed, to 10 mm long. Buds pinkish. Flowers white with pink sepals, solitary, about 12 mm across, with hairy floral tube. Woody fruit capsules, to 6 mm across, are covered with soft hairs.

Flowering period	Nov. to Jan.
Distribution	Widespread on sandstone areas of the Sydney district and in many areas of the State; also Qld.
Habitat	Woodland and heath, especially on exposed rocky sites.
Notes	The name 'arachnoides' means 'spider-like', referring to the creeping habit of this species.
Similar species	None in the region.
Specific sites	Sphinx–Bobbin Head, Waterfall–Uloola Falls, Curra Moors (Royal NP).

Family Myrtaceae

Description

Erect or spreading shrub, to 2 m tall, with smooth hard bark. Leaves narrow, incurved, pungent-pointed, to 15 mm long; they are without a stalk and tend to be held erect on the branches. Flowers white, solitary, about 10 mm across, with hairless floral tube. Fruit a woody capsule, to 7 mm across.

Flowering period	Irregular, but mainly Oct. to Dec.
Distribution	Scattered around Sydney, extending to Blue Mountains. Occurs along coast and tablelands of NSW; also Qld.
Habitat	Swamps, wet heath and scrubby banks of streams, in sandy soil.
Notes	The name 'juniperinum' is a reference to the sharp juniper-like leaves.
Similar species	*L. continentale* has leaves which are more spreading and have a distinctive broad stalk.
Specific sites	Maddens Plains, Goarra Rill (Engadine), Curra Moors (Royal NP).

Family Myrtaceae

Description

Large spreading shrub or small tree, with greyish bark shed in strips. Old trees may reach 6–8 m in height, but most are shorter than 4 m. Leaves broadly obtuse, grey-green, thick, with a small pointed apex, to 2 cm long. Flowers white, about 15 mm across, and borne in the leaf axils. Fruit a woody capsule with 8–12 valves.

Flowering period	Late July to Oct.
Distribution	Coastline, usually within salt spray zone. Occurs all along NSW coast; also Vic, SA and Tas.
Habitat	Sand dunes and coastal headlands.
Notes	A common species in landscaping, dune rehabilitation and coastal gardens.
Similar species	None in the region.
Specific sites	Kurnell, Maroubra, La Perouse, Long Reef (Collaroy).

Family Myrtaceae

Description

Upright shrub, to 4 m tall, with hard bark. Leaves narrow elliptic, tapering at the apex and base, to 2 cm long. Flowers white with green centres, about 15 mm across, borne abundantly at the ends of slender branchlets. Buds often appearing yellowish. Fruit a hairless woody capsule, 6–8 mm across, with 5 valves.

Flowering period	Oct. to Dec.
Distribution	Widespread and common in Sydney district, extending to Blue Mountains and Southern Highlands; also south coast and southern tablelands of NSW.
Habitat	Creek banks and wet heath, usually in deep sandy soil.
Notes	The former name for this species, *L. flavescens*, was a reference to the yellowish appearance of some plants.
Similar species	None in the region.
Specific sites	Castlereagh NR, Flat Rock Creek (Royal NP), Devlins Creek (North Epping).

Family Myrtaceae

Description

Shrub, to 3 m tall, with hard bark and pungent lance-shaped leaves,
to 15 mm long. Flowers white to pink, with a pink-red centre,
about 16 mm across, and are borne singly but abundantly along the
old wood. Fruit is a hairless domed capsule, about 12 mm across,
with 5 valves.

Flowering period	Dec. to April; a few flowers at other times.
Distribution	Widespread on sandstone areas of the Sydney district, extending to Blue Mountains and Southern Highlands; also south coast and southern tablelands of NSW.
Habitat	Scrub and heath, usually in sandy soil.
Notes	A common species, conspicuous because of its massed display of pink flowers in summer and autumn.
Similar species	None in the region.
Specific sites	Loftus Heights, Waterfall–Uloola Falls, Curra Moors (Royal NP).

Family Myrtaceae

Description

Spreading untidy shrub, to 4 m tall, with distinctive flaky bark on
trunk and branches. Leaves variable, broad linear to elliptic, to
20 mm x 5 mm, with 3 longitudinal veins, sometimes faint.
Broad-leaf and narrow-leaf forms are recognised varieties. Flowers
white, about 12 mm across, with a hairy floral tube. Fruit a woody
hairy capsule, to 6 mm across, with 4–5 valves. Unlike most
tea-trees, this fruit is not retained on the plant for a long time.

Flowering period	Oct. to Nov.
Distribution	Widespread and common on sandstone areas of Sydney district, and along most of the coast and tablelands of NSW; also Qld and Vic.
Habitat	Woodland, heath and scrub, in sandy soil.
Notes	A very variable species in its habit and leaf shape, but always recognisable by its flaky bark.
Similar species	*L. grandifolium* also has peeling, flaky bark and hairy floral tube, but its fruit is hairless and it is only found along rocky streams.
Specific sites	Mona Vale, Castlereagh NR, Devlins Creek (North Epping), Waterfall–Uloola Falls.

Family Epacridaceae

Description

Straggling shrub, with weak branches, to 80 cm long. Leaves roughly heart-shaped, to 25 mm x 20 mm, with stem–clasping bases and a fringe of hairs along the margins. Flowers small, white, densely hairy inside and borne on spikes to 30 cm long. Fruit is a small fleshy berry.

Flowering period	Aug. to Oct.
Distribution	Coast and lower Blue Mountains in sandstone areas. Extending south along coast to Shoalhaven district.
Habitat	Sheltered rocky areas in forest and woodland.
Notes	Previously listed on the national rare and endangered list, but now thought to be adequately protected in Sydney's national parks.
Similar species	None in the region.
Specific sites	Cowan Creek, Muogamarra, Woronora River, Oatley Park.

Family Epacridaceae

Description

Small prickly shrub, to 80 cm tall, with soft-hairy branchlets. Leaves spreading, narrow, to 10 mm long, sharp pointed and with margins curled under. Buds pink; flowers white, erect, hairy inside and borne in small clusters of 3–8 in the leaf axils.

Flowering period	July to Oct.
Distribution	Widespread in the Sydney district, extending to Blue Mountains; also coastal and tablelands zones of NSW, Vic and Tas.
Habitat	Woodland and heath, in sand and sandy clay soils.
Notes	The generic name is derived from Greek words for 'white' and 'beard', a reference to the hairy flowers.
Similar species	*L. juniperinus* has fewer flowers and more compact leaves.
Specific sites	Kurnell, Agnes Banks NR, Castlereagh NR, Devlins Creek (North Epping).

Family Epacridaceae

Description

Small erect prickly shrub, to 1 m tall, with many small branchlets and a dense covering of small pungent leaves, to 10 mm long. These leaves are finely toothed and margins are curled under. Flowers white, solitary, with a tube to 6 mm long, hairy inside. Flowers usually borne on older branches.

Flowering period	July to Oct.
Distribution	Widespread in the Sydney district and along coastal and tablelands zones of NSW; also Qld and Vic.
Habitat	Open forest, woodland and shrubland, in both clay and sandy soils.
Notes	A dense shrub with very prickly leaves, supposedly resembling those of the European juniper.
Similar species	*L. ericoides* is a more open shrub with more flowers along the stems.
Specific sites	Kurnell, Oatley Park, Lansdowne Park, Devlins Creek (North Epping).

185

Leucopogon lanceolatus   Lance-leaf Beard–heath

Family Epacridaceae

Description

Erect bushy shrub, to 2 m tall, with flat, lance-shaped leaves, to 4 cm long. Flowers white, hairy inside and borne in loose spikes which may be longer than the leaves. Fruit a rounded fleshy berry, becoming red when ripe.

Flowering period	Sept. to Dec.
Distribution	Widespread in the Sydney district and throughout much of the State; also Qld, Vic, SA and Tas.
Habitat	Forest and margins of rainforest, in shaded sites and in a variety of soils.
Notes	Ripe red fruits are succulent and are eaten by birds, especially rosellas.
Similar species	None in the region.
Specific sites	Helensburgh, Devlins Creek (North Epping), Curra Moors (Royal NP).

Family Epacridaceae

Description

Erect or spreading small shrub, to 60 cm tall, with tiny ovate leaves crowded and upright along the stems; leaves mostly 2–4 mm long, occasionally to 7 mm long. Flowers white, hairy inside and borne in small clusters at the ends of the branchlets.

Flowering period	Mainly May to Nov., but some flowers at other times.
Distribution	Widespread and common on sandstone areas of Sydney district. Extending to Blue Mountains and along coastal and tablelands zones of NSW; also Qld.
Habitat	Heath and dry open forest, in sandy soil.
Notes	The common and botanical names are aptly descriptive.
Similar species	None in the region.
Specific sites	Lane Cove NP, Waterfall–Uloola Falls, Poulton Park (Oatley Bay).

Family Epacridaceae

Description

Erect shrub, mostly to 1.5 m tall, occasionally larger. Leaves lance-shaped, to 2 cm long, paler below, either flat or with margins slightly rolled under. Flowers white, hairy inside and borne in dense spikes which are shorter than the leaves. Fruit a round fleshy berry, white when ripe.

Flowering period	July to Sept.
Distribution	Along the coast near the sea. Extending all along the NSW coast; also all Australian states, NZ and Lord Howe Is.
Habitat	Sand dunes and nearby coastal scrub.
Notes	Fruits edible and attract rosellas and other birds.
Similar species	None in the region.
Specific sites	Avalon, Maroubra, Cronulla, Towra Point.

Family Arecaceae

Description

Tall tree with a single stem, to 30 m tall, topped by large leaves
clustered in a terminal crown. Leaves fan-shaped, to 4 m long and
1 m across, deeply divided into numerous segments. Spines occur at
the leaf base. Many small yellow flowers are borne in an
inflorescence up to 1 m long, followed by globular black fleshy
fruit, to 15 mm diameter.

Flowering period	Aug. to Dec.
Distribution	Scattered along coastal zone north and south of Sydney. Occurs all along NSW coast; also Qld and Vic.
Habitat	Sheltered slopes and gullies, and rainforest margins.
Notes	Growing tip was eaten as 'cabbage' by Aborigines and early white settlers. Settlers also wove leaves into hats and used stems for building.
Similar species	*Archontophoenix cunninghamiana* is the only other palm in the region; it has long, not fan-shaped, leaves.
Specific sites	Kurnell Nature Walk, Bilgola, Palm Jungle (Royal NP).

Family Lobeliaceae

Description

Creeping to erect herb, to 50 cm tall, with distinctly angled stems. Leaves scattered, variable in size and shape, mostly narrow elliptic, to 5 cm long, with slightly toothed margins. Flowers blue to whitish, with 2 narrow upper lobes and 3 spreading lower lobes. Flowers borne singly on stalks shorter than the leaves.

Flowering period	Nov. to March.
Distribution	Coastline and margins of inlets, with a few records from Blue Mountains. Occurs all along coast of NSW, in all other States, South Africa and South America.
Habitat	Saltmarsh, seepages near sea cliffs and around wet rocks of rainforest.
Notes	A small plant which is very tolerant of salt spray and saline conditions.
Similar species	None in the region.
Specific sites	Wattamolla, Pearl Beach, Oatley Park, Curra Moors (Royal NP).

Family Lobeliaceae

Description

Erect or weak herb, with branched stems, to 30 cm long. Leaves scattered, lanceolate to linear, deeply toothed to entire. Flowers deep blue, with 3 large lower petals; the middle petal is larger and rounded, the lateral petals narrow. Flower centre is white and yellow. Flowers borne on slender stalks along an extended inflorescence. Fruit a rounded capsule, to 4 mm long, swollen on the upper surface.

Flowering period	Nov. to May.
Distribution	Coastal zone north of Royal NP to Hawkesbury River. Occurs along north coast, northern tablelands and north west slopes of NSW; also Qld.
Habitat	Open forest and woodland, in sandy soil.
Notes	Grows and flowers quickly after fire, probably from seed stored in the ground.
Similar species	*L. dentata* and *L. gibbosa* have flowers in which the 3 lower petals are all narrow.
Specific sites	Jannali Park, Oatley Park, Maroota–Sackville.

Family Loganiaceae

Description

Erect shrub, to 2 m tall, with opposite, flat, lance-shaped leaves, to 5 cm long, paler on the undersurface. Flowers small, white, tubular, 2–3 mm long, and borne abundantly in inflorescences about 2 cm long from the leaf axils.

Flowering period	June to Oct.
Distribution	Widespread in the Sydney district and throughout much of the State; also Qld, Vic and Lord Howe Is.
Habitat	Open forest, on slopes and in gullies.
Notes	A striking shrub when fully in flower. Male and female flowers are borne on different plants.
Similar species	None in the region.
Specific sites	Bobbin Head, Katandra Reserve, Devlins Creek (North Epping), Curra Moors (Royal NP).

Family Proteaceae

Description

Shrub, to 1.5 m tall, with leaves deeply divided twice or three times. The whole leaf to 30 cm long; leaf segments narrow, with margins toothed. Small white flowers, about 15 mm long, are borne on long flower stalks well above the leaves. Fruit a leathery follicle splitting to reveal several flat seeds in two rows with yellow powder between the seeds.

Flowering period	Dec. to Feb.
Distribution	Widespread on sandstone areas in the Sydney district, extending to Blue Mountains and northern parts of the State; also Qld.
Habitat	Open forest, woodland and heath, in sandy soil.
Notes	Flowers similar to those of *Grevillea*, but differing in the number of seeds. *Grevillea* has two seeds in the follicle, *Lomatia* has more than two.
Similar species	None in the region.
Specific sites	Darkes Forest, Bents Basin, Oatley Park, Curra Moors (Royal NP).

Lyperanthus suaveolens **Brown Beaks**

Family Orchidaceae

Description

Small terrestrial orchid with upright stems, to 40 cm tall. Leaf solitary at the base of the stem, erect, leathery, dark green above, whitish below, to 20 cm long. Flowers 2–6 in terminal inflorescence, reddish brown with yellow centre, to 3 cm across. Flower segments narrow, with petals erect, lateral sepals downcurved and dorsal sepal curved over the column.

Flowering period	Aug. to Nov.
Distribution	Scattered and infrequent in the Sydney district. Occurs all along NSW coast and into central tablelands and western slopes; also Qld, Vic and Tas.
Habitat	Open forest, woodland and scrub, in sandy soil.
Notes	Flowers are fragrant, hence the name 'suaveolens' ('suavis' is Latin for 'sweet').
Similar species	None in the region.
Specific sites	Castlereagh NR, Oatley Park, La Perouse.

Family Zamiaceae

Description

Palm-like dioecious plant with a crown of long leathery leaves
rising from a subterranean trunk. Leaves to 2 m long, divided into
leaflets which are sharp-tipped, thick, rigid, to 20 cm long. Both
male and female cone cylindrical, to 45 cm long and 20 cm wide.
Ripe cones break open to reveal orange-red fruit, 2–3 cm diameter.

Flowering period	Cones produced at irregular intervals, often following bushfire.
Distribution	Widespread in the Sydney district; also north coast and south coast of NSW, and Qld.
Habitat	Sheltered forest, in sandy soil.
Notes	Fruit poisonous, but eaten by Aboriginal people after they roasted the seeds and leached out the toxins.
Similar species	*M. spiralis* is much smaller and occurs mainly in western Sydney.
Specific sites	Kurnell, Palm Beach, Oatley Park.

Family Myrtaceae

Description

Shrub or small tree, to 5 m tall, with hard bark. Leaves narrow
linear, alternate, to 25 mm x 1 mm, usually with a downcurved apex
and an acute but not pungent tip. Flowers white, in a dense flower
spike to 6 cm long, followed by clusters of oblong woody fruit,
about 5 mm diameter.

Flowering period	Sept. to Nov.
Distribution	Scattered along narrow coastal zone north and south of Sydney. Widely distributed in the State; also Qld, Vic and Tas.
Habitat	Scrub and heath, often on coastal headlands, in sandy soil.
Notes	A species which sometimes dominates coastal zones. Widely planted beside roads.
Similar species	*M. ericifolia* has leaves scattered or in whorls of 3.
Specific sites	Kurnell, North Head, Curracurrong (Royal NP).

Family Myrtaceae

Description

Shrub, to 2 m tall, with hard bark. Leaves narrow linear to terete, alternate, to 12 mm x 0.5 mm, usually with a downcurved apex and an acute but not pungent tip. Flowers rosy-pink, in a dense flower spike, to 4 cm long, followed by clusters of oblong woody fruit, about 3 mm diam.

Flowering period	Nov. to Jan.
Distribution	Scattered in western Sydney. Chiefly a species of western slopes and plains of NSW; also Qld.
Habitat	Woodland, in clay soil.
Notes	The name 'erubescens' is derived from the Latin for 'blushing' or 'reddening' ('rubere'), a reference to its rosy pink flowers.
Similar species	None in the region.
Specific sites	Rookwood Cemetery, Castlereagh NR, Windsor Downs NR.

Family Myrtaceae

Description

Medium to large shrub, 2–5 m tall, with corky bark. Leaves lance-shaped, opposite to 3 cm x 1 cm. Flowers red, in dense flower spikes, to 5 cm long, borne on the lower parts of branches and followed by clusters of ovoid woody fruit, to 10 mm diam., crowned by erect teeth.

Flowering period	Nov. to Feb.
Distribution	Scattered along coastal zone, especially near sea, but extending to Blue Mountains and Southern Highlands; also south coast and southern tablelands of NSW.
Habitat	Heath, coastal headlands and gullies, usually in damp sandy soil.
Notes	A popular shrub in cultivation, often planted along roadsides and in council landscaping.
Similar species	None in the region.
Specific sites	Barrenjoey, Audley, Palm Jungle Track (Royal NP).

Melaleuca linariifolia

Family Myrtaceae

Description

Bushy or spreading tree, to 10 m tall, with papery bark. Leaves narrow lanceolate, to 40 mm x 3 mm, with apex acute but not pungent. Flowers white, in abundant fluffy bundles, to 4 cm long, with up to 60 prominent stamens in each bundle. Fruit in clusters, each a rounded woody capsule, to 3 mm diameter.

Flowering period	Oct. to Jan.
Distribution	Scattered in the Sydney district. Occurs along most of coast and tablelands of NSW; also Qld.
Habitat	Floodplains, in sandy alluvium.
Notes	A paperbark tree which yields valuable essential oils.
Similar species	None in the region.
Specific sites	Castlereagh NR, Windsor Downs NR, Scheyville NP.

Family Myrtaceae

Description

Spreading shrub, to 3 m tall, with corky bark. Leaves needle-like, alternate, rigid and pungent-pointed, to 20 mm x 2 mm. Flowers yellow, in dense rounded heads, about 15 mm diameter, followed by rounded clusters of woody fruit which are retained on the plant for several years.

Flowering period	Sept. to Nov.
Distribution	Widespread and common in the Sydney district, and in many areas of the State; also Qld and SA.
Habitat	Woodland and heath, usually in clay or shale soils, but also in sandstone areas.
Notes	A small prickly shrub which forms thickets in some areas.
Similar species	None in the region.
Specific sites	Kurnell, Shanes Park, La Perouse, Rookwood Cemetery.

Family Myrtaceae

Description

Shrub, to 3 m tall, with corky bark. Leaves lance-shaped, crowded and pointed, upright along the stem, apex acute, with 3–5 longitudinal veins, to 10 mm x 3 mm. Flowers pink to mauve, in dense rounded heads, about 2 cm diameter. These are followed by tight clusters of woody fruit, each about 7 mm diameter.

Flowering period	July to Nov.
Distribution	Scattered north and south of Sydney, extending to higher Blue Mountains; also NSW north coast, Vic, SA and Tas.
Habitat	Wet heath and creek banks.
Notes	An attractive shrub with pink pom-pom flowers.
Similar species	None in the region.
Specific sites	Upper O'Hares Creek (Darkes Forest), La Perouse, Curra Moors (Royal NP).

Family Myrtaceae

Description

Spreading shrub, to 1.5 m tall, with corky bark. Leaves narrow, elliptic, opposite, apex acute, to 12 mm x 3 mm. Flowers deep mauve, with curled stamens, in spikes to 2 cm long, with only a few flowers borne on the older wood. Fruit a barrel–shaped woody capsule, to 5 mm diameter, topped by spreading teeth.

Flowering period	Oct. to Jan.
Distribution	Widespread in the Sydney district and in many areas of the State; also Qld.
Habitat	Open forest and woodland, in damp clay, shale and sandy soil.
Notes	A dainty shrub with clusters of mauve flowers.
Similar species	None in the region.
Specific sites	Castlereagh NR, Windsor Downs NR, Agnes Banks NR, Oatley Park.

Micromyrtus ciliata   **Fringed Heath–myrtle**

Family Myrtaceae

Description

Low spreading shrub, seldom more than 1 m tall, with tiny crowded
leaves, to 4 mm long, dotted with oil glands. These leaves have
minute hairs ('ciliate') along the margins, but the leaf keel is hairless.
Flowers white, with small tube to 2 mm long, and 5 spreading
petals, to 4 mm long, stalkless and borne abundantly in showy
terminal heads.

Flowering period	Aug. to Sept.
Distribution	Widespread on sandstone areas of the Sydney district and in many areas of the State; also Vic and SA.
Habitat	Woodland and heath, on rocky sites.
Notes	Abundant tiny white flowers make this small plant quite conspicuous.
Similar species	*M. minutiflora* has flowers on a tiny stalk; it is found in Castlereagh area of western Sydney. *M. blakelyi* has leaves with ciliate keel; it is restricted to Muogamarra NR and Maroota areas.
Specific sites	Sphinx–Bobbin Head, Kurnell, La Perouse.

Family Fabaceae

Description

Small sprawling shrub, mostly ground-hugging, seldom more than 30 cm tall. Leaves in whorls of 3, lance-shaped, to 25 mm long, pungent pointed and with conspicuous small veins on the upper surface. Flowers pink to mauve-purple, in clusters from leaf axils, followed by an inflated ovoid pod, to 5 mm long.

Flowering period	Sept. to Nov.
Distribution	Widespread on sandstone areas of the Sydney district, extending to Blue Mountains. Occurs all along coast and tablelands of NSW; also Qld.
Habitat	Open forest, woodland and heath, usually in sandy soils.
Notes	Easily overlooked when not in flower because of its small size.
Similar species	None in the region.
Specific sites	Castlereagh NR, Scheyville NP, Curra Moors (Royal NP).

Family Fabaceae

Description

Erect shrub, to 80 cm tall. Leaves in whorls of 3, narrow linear, to 3 cm long, with a short pungent point. Flowers purple with a yellow centre, to 12 mm long, becoming blue as they die. They are borne singly from upper leaf axils and are followed by an inflated ovoid pod, to 10 mm long.

Flowering period   July to Aug.

Distribution   Scattered along coast and nearby plateaux, but more common south of Sydney; also northern tablelands of NSW and Qld.

Habitat   Heath and woodland, in sandy soil.

Notes   An uncommon plant, but one which attracts attention because of its purple flowers borne in winter months.

Similar species   None in the region.

Specific sites   Waterfall–Uloola Falls, O'Hares Creek (Darkes Forest), West Head (Ku-ring-gai Chase), Picnic Point.

Family Loganiaceae

Description

Erect to diffuse perennial, to 25 cm tall, with many slender branches
often covered with long soft or sandpapery hairs. Leaves variable,
mostly narrow ovate, to 12 mm long, with a hairy surface. Flowers
white, with bell-shaped tube and 4 rounded spreading lobes.
Flowers borne on the ends of thin stalks, to 10 cm long , with up to
6 flowers in each inflorescence.

Flowering period	Aug. to Jan.
Distribution	Widespread and common on sandstone areas in the Sydney district. Occurs all along NSW coast and tablelands; also Qld, Vic and Tas.
Habitat	Open forest, woodland and heath.
Notes	The generic name is a reference to the supposed similarity of the flower to the top of a bishop's tall cap. The specific name 'polymorpha' means 'many forms', a reference to the varied leaf shapes.
Similar species	None in the region.
Specific sites	Castlereagh NR, Agnes Banks NR, Curra Moors (Royal NP).

Family Epacridaceae

Description

Compact shrub to small tree, usually 2–4 m tall, with old trees much taller. Leaves elliptic, spreading, dark green above, grey-glaucous below, to 25 mm x 6 mm. Flowers creamy-white, with small (2 mm) bell-shaped tube and spreading lobes, borne in inflorescences near the ends of branches. Fruit fleshy, ovoid, orange-red, to 4 mm long.

Flowering period	Aug. to Sept.
Distribution	Widespread, but especially common near the sea and tidal estuaries. Extending to Blue Mountains; also coastal and tablelands zones of the State, Qld, Vic and Tas.
Habitat	Low open forest, cliff tops near ocean and coastal sand dunes.
Notes	A slow growing and long lived species. Large old plants usually in unburnt areas.
Similar species	None in the region.
Specific sites	Kurnell, La Perouse, Oatley Park, Curra Moors (Royal NP).

Family Myoporaceae

Description

Erect shrub, to 2 m tall, with hairless branches. Leaves obovate to elliptic, shiny, with an apex broadly acute, to 5 cm x 3 cm. Flowers white, unspotted, on stalks to 15 mm long and borne in clusters of 1–8 in the leaf axils. Fruit fleshy, rounded, light purple, to 8 mm diameter.

Flowering period	March to Aug.
Distribution	Coastal zone, north and south of Sydney; also south coast, north coast and Qld.
Habitat	Coastal heath and scrub, especially on rocky sea cliffs and along sandy inlets.
Notes	Easily identified by its white flowers and fleshy pale purple berries.
Similar species	Previously confused with *M. insulare*, a species which does not occur in the Sydney area. *M. acuminatum* has larger leaves with pointed apex and purple spotted flowers.
Specific sites	Castlecove, Mona Vale, Minnamurra Spit.

Family Oleaceae

Description

Spreading shrub to small tree, to 7 m tall, with greyish bark and
stems with white lenticels (raised spots). Young stems, flower stalks
and undersurface of leaves usually softly hairy, but older leaves often
hairless and leathery. Leaves opposite, broadly ovate, to 10 cm
x 4 cm, with distinct reticulated veins. Small yellowish flowers
borne in racemes from leaf axils, followed by blue-black ovoid fruit.

Flowering period	April to July.
Distribution	Widespread in the Sydney district. Occurs along the coast, tablelands and central western slopes of NSW.
Habitat	Open forest, in both sandy and clay soils.
Notes	This species belongs to the same family as the European olive and bears olive-like fruit.
Similar species	*N. venosa* has leaves with finely reticulate veins and ellipsoid fruit.
Specific sites	North Head, Kurnell, Bola Creek (Royal NP).

Family Olacaceae

Description

Erect yellow-green shrub, to 1.5 m tall. Leaves linear to narrow elliptic, to 10 mm long, with apex pointed and downturned, arranged in two rows on opposite sides of the stems. Flowers white to yellow, with 5 petals, about 5 mm long, borne singly in the leaf axils. These are followed by an ellipsoid fleshy fruit.

Flowering period	Some flowers all year round.
Distribution	Widespread in the Sydney district, and in many areas of the State; also Qld and Vic.
Habitat	Woodland and heath, in sandy soil.
Notes	This species is semi-parasitic on the roots of nearby plants.
Similar species	None in the region.
Specific sites	Engadine (Royal NP), Sphinx (North Turramurra), Agnes Banks NR.

Family Asteraceae

Description

Upright, much-branched shrub, to 3 m tall, with small crowded leaves, to 15 mm long; leaf margins are curled under and undersurface is woolly white. Flowers small and white, only 2–3 mm across, but are borne in numerous dense flower heads.

Flowering period	Oct. to Dec.
Distribution	Widespread in the Sydney district and throughout much of the State; also Qld.
Habitat	Open forest, especially in fertile clay soils but sometimes sandy soil.
Notes	Formerly classified as a *Helichrysum*, this tall shrub is conspicuous when flowering.
Similar species	This species may be confused with *Cassinia trinervia*, also a shrub with white flower heads. However, *C. trinervia* has longer 3-veined leaves.
Specific sites	Otford, Agnes Banks NR, Castlereagh NR, Pennant Hills Park.

Family Iridaceae

Description

Erect leafy plant, 30–50 cm tall. Leaves narrow, flat, hairless, mostly 10–40 cm long, and borne along the upright stem. Pale violet flowers with 3 rounded petal-like lobes borne on hairless stems to 30 cm long. Flowers backed by a spathe bract, which is brown, sparsely silky to hairless, to 6 cm long, enclosing up to 6 flowers which open in succession on sunny days.

Flowering period	Sept. to Nov.
Distribution	Widespread in coastal sands in the Sydney district, extending to Blue Mountains. Occurs along most of NSW coast and tablelands; also Qld.
Habitat	Open forest, woodland and heath, in sandy soil.
Notes	The only species of *Patersonia* in the Sydney district which has leaves along the stems and not arising from base of the plant.
Similar species	None in the region.
Specific sites	O'Hares Creek, Oatley Park, Pennant Hills Park.

Family Iridaceae

Description

Small perennial, to 50 cm tall, with strap-like linear leaves rising as a clump from ground level, to 50 cm long and 3–5 mm wide. Violet flowers with 3 rounded petal-like lobes borne on stems to 55 cm long. Flowers are backed by a spathe bract, which is dark brown to black and silky hairy, to 6 cm long, enclosing up to 6 flowers which open in succession on sunny days.

Flowering period	July to Dec.
Distribution	Widespread in the Sydney district, extending to the Blue Mountains. Occurs in most areas of the State; also Qld and Vic.
Habitat	Open forest, woodland and heath, in sandy soil.
Notes	The name 'sericea' is a reference to the silky spathe enclosing the flowers.
Similar species	*P. longifolia* has leaves 1–2 mm wide with a row of hairs along the margins. *P. fragilis* is hairless, with flower stalks much shorter than the leaves.
Specific sites	Engadine (Royal NP), Castlereagh NR, Windsor Downs NR.

Family Proteaceae

Description

Medium shrub, to 2 m tall, with lance-shaped leaves, erect to
spreading, to 7 cm x 2 cm, light green with only the mid-vein
prominent. Flowers yellow, tubular, with 4 recurved segments, on
short (1–2 mm) stalks from the leaf axils. Fruit a green ovoid drupe.

Flowering period	Mainly March to July; some flowers at other times.
Distribution	Widespread on coastal sandstone areas in the Sydney district. Also scattered along north coast, south coast and central tablelands of NSW.
Habitat	Open forest and scrub, especially in deep coastal sand.
Notes	The name 'geebung' refers to the fleshy fruit which in some species is edible.
Similar species	None in the region.
Specific sites	Kurnell, Engadine–Waterfall, Scheyville NP.

Family Proteaceae

Description

Spreading shrub, to 1 m tall, with dense hairy young branches.
Leaves opposite, ovate, to 10 cm x 6 cm, either smooth or
sandpapery above and lighter below. Flowers yellow, tubular, with
4 recurved segments and densely covered with rust-coloured hairs.
They are borne on short (1–2 mm) hairy stalks from the leaf axils.
Fruit a green ovoid drupe.

Flowering period	Oct. to Dec.
Distribution	Widespread but uncommon in the Sydney district. Occurs along most of NSW coast and tablelands.
Habitat	Open forest and heath, in sandy and clay-shale soils.
Notes	Young branches and the outside of the flowers are densely hairy.
Similar species	None in the region.
Specific sites	Oatley Park, Agnes Banks NR, Curra Moors (Royal NP).

Family Proteaceae

Description

Erect or crooked shrub, to 4 m tall, with loose flaky bark, red
beneath the dark outer surface. Young branches often reddish.
Leaves variable, broad elliptical to sickle-shaped, to 15 cm x 6 cm.
Flowers yellow, tubular, with 4 recurved segments, on short
(3–6 mm) stalks from the leaf axils. Fruit a green ovoid drupe.

Flowering period	July to Dec.
Distribution	Widespread and common on sandstone areas of the Sydney district. Occurs along most of NSW coast and tablelands; also Vic.
Habitat	Open forest, woodland and heath, in sandy soil.
Notes	This species is easily identified because of its large light green leaves and flaky bark.
Similar species	None in the region.
Specific sites	Kurnell, Engadine–Waterfall, Sphinx (North Turramurra), Oatley Park.

Family Proteaceae

Description

Erect to spreading shrub or small tree, to 5 m tall, with flaky bark.
Leaves linear, to 8 cm x 0.6 cm. Flowers yellow, tubular, with 4
recurved segments, on short (2–6 mm) hairy stalks from leaf axils.
Fruit a globular drupe, green with dark stripes.

Flowering period	Dec. to July.
Distribution	Widespread throughout the Sydney district. Occurs all along coast and tablelands of NSW; also Vic.
Habitat	Open forest and woodland.
Notes	The bark of this species peels in thin tissue-like layers.
Similar species	*P. levis* also has flaky bark, but has much wider leaves.
Specific sites	Oatley Park, Castlereagh NR, Bents Basin, Forest Island (Royal NP).

Family Proteaceae

Description

Large spreading shrub, to 4 m tall, with crowded needle-like leaves, to 5 cm long, with non-pungent tips. Flowers yellow, tubular, with 4 recurved segments, borne in a dense terminal raceme, to 15 cm long which is usually pendulous. Fruits globular, green turning purple.

Flowering period	March to July.
Distribution	Restricted to coastal sandstone areas of Sydney from Broken Bay to Waterfall; extending to lower Blue Mountains.
Habitat	Open forest and woodland, often on protected sandy slopes.
Notes	The fruits of this species hang like bunches of grapes from tips of branchlets.
Similar species	None in the region.
Specific sites	Sphinx (North Turramurra), Curra Moors Track (Royal NP), Kellys Falls (Otford).

Family Proteaceae

Description

Erect shrub, to 2.5 m tall, with softly hairy young growth. Leaves much divided into narrow, terete, rigid, somewhat pungent segments; new growth often reddish. Flowers yellow, in ovoid, stalkless, cone-like structures, 2–3 cm long. Fruit a small hairy nut, only 3 mm long, held in a woody cone-like structure.

Flowering period	Dec. to Jan.
Distribution	Widespread south of Sydney in coastal sandstone zone; also Agnes Banks. Extending to south coast and tablelands of the State.
Habitat	Open forest, scrub and heath, on sandy or rocky sites.
Notes	The genus name means 'rock lover' from the Greek 'petra' and 'philo', but this species is more commonly found in sandy soil.
Similar species	*P. pulchella* does not have the rigid pungent leaves.
Specific sites	Agnes Banks NR, O'Hares Creek (Darkes Forest), Engadine–Waterfall.

Family Rutaceae

Description

Erect or spreading shrub, to 2 m tall, more or less covered with
brown scales on stems, buds and back of flowers. Leaves narrow
oblong, to 5 cm x 1 cm, hairless above, lower surface silvery and
with rust-coloured scales. Flowers yellow to almost white, with
5 star-like petals and 10 free stamens, each flower on stalks to
8 mm long and borne in terminal clusters.

Flowering period	Aug. to Nov.
Distribution	Widespread on sandstone areas in the Sydney district, and throughout much of the State; also Qld and Vic.
Habitat	Open forest, woodland and heath, on sandy and rocky sites.
Notes	The name 'squamulosum' means 'scaly', a reference to the rust-like scales which are a feature of this plant.
Similar species	Ssp. *argenteum* has oblong leaves with rounded apex and silvery scales underneath; its flowers are cream.
Specific sites	Warrah Sanct. (Patonga), Flat Rock Creek (Royal NP), Bents Basin (Nepean River).

Family Rutaceae

Description

Small spreading shrub, to 1 m tall, with prominent oil glands on stems and leaves. Leaves rounded to elliptic, to 15 mm x 12 mm, with pointed apex and lower surface distinctly keeled and tuberculate. Flowers 5-petalled, pink in bud, turning white, borne singly on short stalks from leaf axils along the upper stems.

Flowering period	July to Nov.
Distribution	Restricted to coastal areas from about Manly to Kurnell; also Jervis Bay.
Habitat	Sandy heath.
Notes	Formerly *Eriostemon buxifolius* and still widely known by that name.
Similar species	Ssp. *obovata* has more warty leaves and is found north of Broken Bay. A similar plant common on heaths of Royal NP may be a hybrid of *P. buxifolia* and *P. scabra*.
Specific sites	Dobroyd Head, North Head, Kurnell.

Family Rutaceae

Description

Spreading shrub, varying from a low dwarf plant on coastal heaths to erect and 1 m tall at Agnes Banks. Leaves crowded, linear, to 12 mm long, dotted with oil glands. Flowers mauve, 5-petalled, with 10 erect stamens, hairy at the top, united into a cage-like structure; 1–3 flowers are borne at the ends of branchlets.

Flowering period	July to Nov.
Distribution	Widespread along coast and west to Blue Mountains; also along coast, tablelands and western slopes of NSW.
Habitat	Heath and woodland, especially in deep sands and on rocky sites.
Notes	Easily identified by its 5-petalled mauve flowers with united white stamens in the centre.
Similar species	None in the region.
Specific sites	Warrah Sanct. (Patonga), Agnes Banks NR, Waterfall–Uloola Falls.

Family Rutaceae

Description

Small shrub, to 60 cm tall, with narrow leaves, to 20 mm x 2 mm, distinctly warty underneath and with apex acute. Flowers 5-petalled, pink in bud, turning white, borne singly on short stalks from leaf axils along upper stems.

Flowering period	Aug. to Nov.
Distribution	Restricted to southern Sydney around Georges River and Heathcote NP.
Habitat	Open forest, woodland and heath, in sandy soil.
Notes	Formerly *Eriostemon scaber* and still widely known by that name.
Similar species	Ssp. *latifolia* has broader leaves and occurs around Bundanoon and south of Nowra.
Specific sites	Oatley Park, Jannali Reserve, Kurnell.

Family Fabaceae

Description

Erect shrub, to 1 m tall, with crowded, narrow, upward pointing leaves, to 15 mm x 1 mm, with margins curled under. Flowers yellow with red centres, 5–10 mm long, borne in dense spikes at or near the ends of the branches. Grey hairs of calyx can be seen between the flowers. Fruit a hairy pod, to 5 mm long.

Flowering period	Aug. to Oct.
Distribution	Widespread and common on sandstone areas in the Sydney district, extending to Blue Mountains. Occurs along most of the coast and tablelands of NSW; also Qld.
Habitat	Woodland and heath, in sandy soil.
Notes	A species often mistaken for a *Pultenaea* or *Dillwynia*, but differing in having large green bracteoles on either side of the calyx.
Similar species	*P. grandiflora* is a larger shrub with larger flowers (12–15 mm); it occurs north of Port Jackson.
Specific sites	Sphinx–Bobbin Head, Engadine, Flat Rock Creek (Royal NP).

Family Thymelaeaceae

Description

Upright shrub, to 1 m tall, with slim, tough, hairless stems. Leaves narrow elliptic, opposite, flat, apex pointed, to 18 mm x 3 mm. Flowers white, with a hairy cylindrical floral tube. Up to 40 flowers are borne in a conspicuous terminal head, backed by 4 ovate green bracts.

Flowering period	Mainly July to Oct.; some flowers at other times.
Distribution	Widespread in the Sydney district, and throughout much of the State; also Qld, Vic, SA and Tas.
Habitat	Open forest, woodland and heath, in sandy soil.
Notes	The white flower heads of this species are a common feature of Sydney's bushland, surviving even in small disturbed bush patches.
Similar species	None in the region.
Specific sites	Castlereagh NR, Oatley Park, Curra Moors (Royal NP).

Family Pittosporaceae

Description

Shrub, to 3 m tall, with broad alternate leaves, to 10 cm x 5 cm, often clustered at the ends of the branches, glossy green above and rust-coloured and hairy below when young. Flowers yellow, bell-shaped, with spreading rounded lobes, scented, to 12 mm long, and borne in terminal clusters. Fruit a warty, orange capsule which splits to reveal numerous reddish seeds.

Flowering period	Sept. to Oct.
Distribution	Widespread in the Sydney district. Occurs along coast, tablelands and central western slopes of the State; also Qld and Vic.
Habitat	Moist forest and rainforest, mainly on richer clay-shale soils.
Notes	The numerous showy red seeds attract birds, and the scented flowers are visited by native and introduced bees.
Similar species	None in the region.
Specific sites	West Pittwater, Mitchell Park (Cattai), Palm Jungle (Royal NP).

Family Pittosporaceae

Description

Shrub to small tree, to 10 m tall, with dark green, shiny, elliptic leaves, to 12 cm x 4 cm. New growth is a lighter green, a contrast to the older darker leaves. Flowers white to cream, bell-shaped, with spreading lobes, scented, to 12 mm long, and borne in terminal clusters. Fruit a smooth, rounded, yellow-orange capsule which splits to reveal numerous sticky red-brown seeds.

Flowering period	Sept. to Oct.
Distribution	Widespread and common in the Sydney district and throughout much of the State; also Qld, Vic, SA and Tas.
Habitat	Moist forests, sheltered slopes and gullies.
Notes	Often dominates the margins of urban bushland where it may become a weed because it shades out other species.
Similar species	None in the region.
Specific sites	Carss Park, Bobbin Head, Oatley Park, Bola Creek (Royal NP).

Family Fabaceae

Description

Erect or spreading shrub, to 2 m tall. Leaves opposite, broad-ovate, with a pointed apex and cordate base, to 5 cm x 2 cm; the upper leaf surface has a conspicuous network of small veins. Flowers yellow with red centres, relatively large, to 15 mm long, borne 2 together from leaf axils. Fruit an oblong pod, 2–4 cm long. A small flowered form occurs in sandy-shale soils along the upper Lane Cove Valley.

Flowering period	Sept. to Oct.
Distribution	Widespread in the Sydney district, extending to Blue Mountains. Occurs along most of coast and tablelands zones of NSW; also Qld, Vic and Tas.
Habitat	Sheltered areas of open forest, in both sand and clay soils.
Notes	The name 'formosum' is derived from the Portuguese for 'beautiful'; the same word origin as for Formosa Island (now Taiwan).
Similar species	None in the region.
Specific sites	Mona Vale, Devlins Creek (North Epping), Scheyville NP, Curra Moors Track (Royal NP).

Family Apiaceae

Description

Erect shrub, to 1.5 m tall. Leaves variable, mostly lance-shaped but sometimes rounded, to 3 cm x 1 cm, with a carrot-like odour when crushed. Small white flowers are borne in compound terminal umbels, up to 3 cm across. Fruit small, about 1.5 mm long, warty and separating into 2 flattened segments.

Flowering period	Dec. to April.
Distribution	Widespread in sandy areas of the Sydney district and throughout much of the State; also Qld and Vic.
Habitat	Open forest and heath, in sandy soil or on rocky slopes.
Notes	This species belongs to the same family as the edible carrot, hence the distinctive carrot smell of the leaves. It needs fire for regrowth from seed.
Similar species	None in the region.
Specific sites	Kurnell, Darkes Forest, North Head, Curra Moors (Royal NP).

Family Apiaceae

Description

Spreading or sprawling shrub, to 1 m tall, with slender stems and narrow linear leaves held upright, to 25 mm long; these have a strong carrot-like odour when crushed. Small white flowers are borne in loose compound terminal umbels, to 2 cm across. Fruit small, about 2 mm long, warty and separating into 2 broad flattened segments.

Flowering period	Dec. to April.
Distribution	Widespread and common in sandy areas of the Sydney district and adjacent ranges; also NSW south coast and Qld.
Habitat	Open forest and woodland, in sandy soil.
Notes	The carrot smell of the crushed leaves is a reminder that this species belongs to a family which includes the cultivated carrot, as well as fennel, parsnip and celery.
Similar species	None in the region.
Specific sites	Castlereagh NR, Oatley Park, Curra Moors (Royal NP).

Family Araliaceae

Description

Erect branched shrub, mostly 2–3 m tall. Leaves with up to 10 pairs of leaflets and a single terminal leaflet. Leaflets broad elliptical, mostly toothed, to 9 cm x 3 cm; lower leaflets are smaller than those above. Flowers insignificant, cream to green, borne in umbels on the ends of long stalks. Fruit a succulent, globose drupe, to 4 mm long, blue when ripe and edible.

Flowering period Dec. to Jan.

Distribution Widespread in the Sydney district and throughout coast and tablelands zones of the State; also Qld and Vic.

Habitat Forests, often in sheltered areas, on heavier soils and on rainforest margins.

Notes Commonly occurs on disturbed ground. Probably spread by birds dropping seeds. Although stems are killed by fire, plant regrows from root suckers.

Similar species None in the region.

Specific sites Devlins Creek (North Epping), Oatley Pleasure Grounds, Mitchell Park (Cattai).

Family Rhamnaceae

Description

Large shrub, mostly 2–3 m tall, with branches, leaf stalks and inflorescences covered with dense rust-coloured hairs. Leaves lance-shaped to ovate, to 8 cm x 2.5 cm, the upper surface dull green and with short bristly hairs, the lower surface with longer rust-coloured hairs. Flowers golden yellow, to 4 mm long, with 5 tiny petals and the floral tube with dense white hairs; they are borne in large conspicuous inflorescences above the leaves.

Flowering period	Aug. to Sept.
Distribution	Widespread in the Sydney district and in many areas of the State; also Qld and Vic.
Habitat	Open forest, in sandy soil or sandstone-shale overlap.
Notes	The various *Pomaderris* are difficult to identify with certainty. This species' leaves have simple hairs above and longer rust-coloured hairs below.
Similar species	*P. ligustrina* and *P. ferruginea* have the upper surface of their leaves hairless.
Specific sites	Menai–Bangor, Oatley Park, Maroota–Sackville.

Family Lobeliaceae

Description

Hairless herb, either ascending or trailing, to 30 cm tall, with alternate, toothed leaves, to 15 mm long; undersurface of leaves purplish. Flowers white to pale pink and mauve with a yellow centre. The tubular corolla is split, with 3 spreading lobes below and 2 smaller lobes above. Flowers borne on slender stalks, to 7 cm long. Fruit is a globose capsule, 3–8 mm long, crowned with calyx teeth.

Flowering period	Nov. to May.
Distribution	Widespread in the Sydney district, extending to coast and tablelands zones of the State; also Qld, Vic and Lord Howe Is.
Habitat	Open forest, woodland and wet heath, usually on shaded damp areas in richer soils.
Notes	The common name is a reference to the long white rhizomes of this species.
Similar species	None in the region.
Specific sites	Castlereagh NR, Windsor Downs NR, Scheyville NP.

Family Orchidaceae

Description

Ground orchid, with a slender flower stalk, to 25 cm tall, and a rosette of stalked ovate leaves, to 3 cm long. Hooded green flowers, to 15 mm long, have white and green stripes and some tan markings and are held upright. Narrow lateral sepals, to 2 cm long, are held erect. Labellum dark brown with a deeply notched apex (a feature of this species).

Flowering period	June to Aug.
Distribution	Coastal areas north and south of Sydney. Also south coast and central western slopes of NSW, Vic, SA and Tas.
Habitat	Sheltered areas of open forest and woodland.
Notes	This orchid is often found in large colonies.
Similar species	*P. curta* has shorter lateral sepals and the apex of the labellum is not strongly notched.
Specific sites	Oatley Park, Carss Park, Scheyville NP.

Family Orchidaceae

Description

Ground orchid, with a slender flowering stalk, to 25 cm tall, and a
rosette of 2–6 stalked ovate leaves, to 10 cm long. Hooded green
flowers, to 35 mm long, have white and brown markings and are
held upright. Lateral sepals short and form a V behind which can be
seen the brownish obtuse labellum, twisted to one side.

Flowering period	July to Sept.
Distribution	Widespread around Sydney and throughout much of the coast, tablelands and western slopes of NSW; also Qld, Vic, SA and Tas.
Habitat	Sheltered slopes and gullies of open forest, often forming large colonies.
Notes	A combination of short lateral sepals and twisted labellum helps separate this species from other greenhoods.
Similar species	*P. hildae* has smaller flowers and a non-twisted labellum; it is uncommon in the Sydney district.
Specific sites	Oatley Park, Mooney Mooney Creek, Devlins Creek (North Epping).

Family Fabaceae

Description

Spreading shrub, to 1 m tall, with very distinctive leaves. They are
linear, concave above, warty, to 20 mm long, with white hairs and
an apex terminated by a needle-like spine. Flowers yellow with red
markings, crowded into dense terminal heads. Long brown stipules
occur among the flowers. Fruit is a swollen pod, to 6 mm long.

Flowering period	Sept. to Oct.
Distribution	Restricted to southern Sydney between Helensburgh and Mt Keira.
Habitat	Woodland and heath, in sandy soil.
Notes	The specific name is a reference to the aristate leaf — one which ends in a short stiff point.
Similar species	None in the region.
Specific sites	Darkes Forest, upper O'Hares Creek.

Pultenaea daphnoides Large-leaf Bush-pea

Family Fabaceae

Description

Erect shrub, to 3 m tall. Leaves alternate, wedge-shaped or obovate, to 3 cm long, with rounded or indented apex, a short pointed tip and lower surface lighter than above. Flowers yellow with dark red centres, crowded into dense terminal heads, 2–3 cm across. Fruit is a flattened pod, to 7 mm long.

Flowering period	Aug. to Nov.
Distribution	Widespread on sandstone areas in the Sydney district, extending to Blue Mountains. Occurs all along coast and tablelands of NSW; also Qld, Vic, SA and Tas.
Habitat	Forests, usually on protected slopes and gullies.
Notes	One of a number of *Pultenaea* with terminal flower heads. The leaf shape is the easiest identification feature of this species.
Similar species	None in the region.
Specific sites	Sphinx (North Turramurra), Oatley Park, Curra Moors (Royal NP).

Family Fabaceae

Description

Erect shrub, to 1 m tall. Stems with soft white hairs covered with brown stipules pressed flat. Leaves crowded, narrow elliptic, mostly concave above, hairy when young, to 12 mm long. Flowers yellow-red with red keel, to 10 mm long, borne in terminal heads or in leafy subterminal inflorescences. Fruit is a swollen pod, to 5 mm long.

Flowering period	Oct. to Feb.
Distribution	Widespread in the Sydney district, extending to Blue Mountains. Occurs along coast and tablelands between Lake Macquarie and far south of NSW.
Habitat	Forest, woodland and heath, in sandy soil.
Notes	A common yellow pea flower with a long flowering period from spring through to summer.
Similar species	None in the region.
Specific sites	Castlereagh NR, Agnes Banks NR, Waterfall–Uloola Falls.

Family Fabaceae

Description

Erect shrub, to 2 m tall, with densely hairy stems. Leaves spoon-shaped, softly hairy, to 13 mm x 5 mm. Flowers yellow, to 15 mm long, and borne in small heads at the ends of short branches. Fruit is a swollen pod, to 6 mm long.

Flowering period	Sept. to Oct.
Distribution	Scattered in north and north-west of Sydney, from Terrey Hills to Ourimbah, and Mangrove Mountain.
Habitat	Open woodland and heath, in sandy soil.
Notes	A local endemic species.
Similar species	Variety *ferruginea* has smaller leaves (to 8 mm x 3 mm) and occurs north-west of Sydney.
Specific sites	Barrenjoey, Maroota–Sackville, Patonga.

Family Fabaceae

Description

Erect, bushy shrub, to 4 m tall. Leaves alternate, linear to narrow obovate, flat, pointed at the apex, to 20 mm x 3 mm. Flowers yellow with red centre, about 10 mm long, borne on short stalks near the ends of branches. Fruit a swollen pod, to 9 mm long.

Flowering period	Aug. to Oct.
Distribution	Widespread and common on sandstone areas in the Sydney district and in many areas of the State; also Qld.
Habitat	Open forest, usually on sheltered hillsides and in gullies.
Notes	A showy species, often dominant under eucalypts.
Similar species	*P. blakelyi* has leaves which are opposite.
Specific sites	Sphinx (North Turramurra), Devlins Creek (North Epping), Bents Basin (Nepean River).

Family Fabaceae

Description

Erect or spreading shrub, to 1 m tall. Leaves alternate, linear to wedge-shaped, blunt or indented at the apex, lighter underneath, mostly 1–2 cm long. Flowers yellow with red centres, 5–10 mm long, borne in small dense terminal heads. Fruit a flattened pod, to 6 mm long.

Flowering period	Aug. to Oct.
Distribution	Widespread in the Sydney district, extending to Blue Mountains and Southern Highlands. Occurs all along coast and tablelands of NSW; also Vic.
Habitat	Woodland and heath, in sandy soil.
Notes	The common name comes from the halo of leaves which surround the flower heads.
Similar species	None in the region.
Specific sites	Kurnell, Oatley Park, Bundeena (Royal NP).

Family Fabaceae

Description

Erect shrub, to 2 m tall, with branches covered with narrow brown appressed stipules, each 10 mm long. Leaves crowded, linear, flat, to 3 cm long, with a pointed tip. Flowers yellow, to 15 mm long, crowded into dense terminal heads, about 3 cm across, surrounded by brown enlarged stipules. Fruit a swollen pod, to 7 mm long.

Flowering period	Aug. to Oct.
Distribution	An endemic Sydney species, extending from Broken Bay to Wollongong.
Habitat	Forest, woodland and heath, in sandy soil, usually on protected slopes.
Notes	Conspicuous brown stipules on the stems and surrounding the flower head are a feature of this species.
Similar species	None in the region.
Specific sites	Sphinx (North Turramurra), Oatley Park, Curra Moors Track (Royal NP).

Pultenaea villosa

Hairy Bush–pea

Family Fabaceae

Description

Spreading shrub, to 1.5 m tall, with softly hairy stems and graceful drooping branchlets. Leaves alternate, narrow oblong, concave above, apex blunt or slightly pointed, to 6 mm x 2 mm. Flowers yellow, to 12 mm long, borne in small clusters at the end of side branches. Fruit a swollen pod, to 6 mm long.

Flowering period	Late Aug. to Oct.
Distribution	Scattered around Sydney, but more common in western Sydney. A coastal species extending from Qld to Vic.
Habitat	Open woodland and scrub, in clay soils, shale or alluvium. Absent from Hawkesbury Sandstone areas.
Notes	This attractive shrub is very conspicuous when in full flower in mid-September.
Similar species	*P. ferruginea* is also a softly hairy shrub, but it has spoon-shaped leaves.
Specific sites	Castlereagh NR, Windsor Downs NR, Rookwood Cemetery, Menai–Lucas Heights.

Family Myrsinaceae

Description

Shrub to small tree, mostly 3–4 m tall. Leaves alternate,
oblanceolate, to 8 cm x 2.5 cm, entire or with a few teeth, shiny on
the upper surface, duller below and with leaf stalks 3–7 mm long.
Flowers small, creamy-white and borne in clusters along older
branches. Fruit a stalked, globose, blue drupe, about 5 mm diameter.

Flowering period	June to Oct.
Distribution	Widespread in the Sydney district. Occurs all along NSW coast, northern tablelands and central western slopes; also Qld.
Habitat	Open forest, littoral rainforest and coastal headlands, usually in enriched soils.
Notes	Characterised by clusters of flowers and fleshy fruit along on older wood.
Similar species	*R. howittiana* has adult leaves entire and leaf stalks 7–20 mm long.
Specific sites	Bobbin Head, Devlins Creek (North Epping), Bola Creek (Royal NP).

Family Euphorbiaceae

Description

Erect or spreading shrub, to 3 m tall, with linear, hairless leaves, to 4 cm long, and margins curled under. Flowers with 6 spreading white petals. Male and female flowers separate but on the same plant, usually in the same cluster. Flowers on slender stalks, about 2 cm long, and borne in terminal clusters. Fruit a rounded capsule, about 12 mm across, covered in short dense spines.

Flowering period	Aug. to Nov.
Distribution	Common in coastal sandstone areas of the Sydney district, extending to Blue Mountains. Occurs along coast and tablelands of NSW; also Qld, Vic, Tas and NT.
Habitat	Woodland, heath and scrubland, in sandy soil.
Notes	Common name is derived from the showy mass of white flowers. 'Ricino-carpus' is a reference to the fact that the fruit of this genus resemble those of castor oil plant (*Ricinus*).
Similar species	None in the region.
Specific sites	Kurnell, Agnes Banks NR, Curra Moors (Royal NP).

245

Family Sterculiaceae

Description

Prostrate shrub, sending stems along the ground to 80 cm long, seldom more than 20 cm tall. Leaves oblong, to 2 cm long, with shallow rounded teeth, strongly wrinkled above and densely hairy below. Flowers pink-white, small, with 5 petals, each 2 mm long, and borne in clusters which are often numerous and conspicuous. Fruit a hairy capsule, to 6 mm long, covered with short bristles.

Flowering period	Aug. to Sept.
Distribution	Chiefly confined to sandstone areas close to the coast from Bouddi NP to Royal NP. Also recorded from Jervis Bay–Shoalhaven district.
Habitat	Coastal heath, in sandy soils or over rocky surfaces.
Notes	A rare species. Growth and flowering seem to be encouraged by fire.
Similar species	None in the region.
Specific sites	Kurnell, Bombi Head (Bouddi NP), Deer Pool Track (Royal NP).

Family Goodeniaceae

Description

Straggling plant, occasionally ascending but seldom more than 50 cm tall, with bristly glandular hairs on stems. Leaves narrow lanceolate, entire or toothed, without stalks, to 5 cm long. Flowers purple, with 5 spreading fan-like petals and yellow-white throat, borne on long stalks from leaf axils.

Flowering period	Sept. to Jan.
Distribution	Widespread on sandstone areas in the Sydney district. Occurs all along coast and tablelands of NSW; also Vic and Qld.
Habitat	Open forest and woodland, in sandy soil.
Notes	Flowers shaped like a spreading fan or the broad fingers of a hand.
Similar species	None in the region.
Specific sites	Agnes Banks NR, Oatley Park, Curra Moors Track (Royal NP).

Family Smilacaceae

Description

Slender climber, with long thin stems which often cover lower
undergrowth and ground cover. Leaves lance-shaped, 3-veined,
apex acute, lower surface glaucous, to 6 cm x 3 cm. Prickles occur
at leaf bases but not on stems. New growth pinkish. Flowers small,
creamy and borne in umbels from leaf axils. Fruit a shiny black
globose berry, to 8 mm diameter.

Flowering period	Oct. to Dec.
Distribution	Widespread in coastal zone of the Sydney district, extending to adjacent ranges. Occurs along NSW coast and northern tablelands; also Qld.
Habitat	Open forest and woodland, on sheltered slopes and in gullies, and rainforest.
Notes	Leaves can be soaked in water to produce an aromatic drink.
Similar species	*S. australis* has prickly stems and leathery leaves with 5 veins.
Specific sites	Bobbin Head, Oatley Park, Palm Jungle (Royal NP).

Family Anthericaceae

Description

Soft low herb, to 50 cm tall, with terete to linear leaves, to 50 cm long, arising from base of the flower stem. Flowers mauve-lilac, with 20 or more flowers clustered at the end of a stalk longer than the leaves. Fruit a 3-lobed capsule, 2–3 mm diameter.

Flowering period	Sept. to Nov.
Distribution	Scattered throughout the Sydney district, extending to Blue Mountains. Occurs along most of NSW coast and tablelands; also Qld and Vic.
Habitat	Damp heaths.
Notes	The delicate flowers have a slight vanilla aroma.
Similar species	None in the region.
Specific sites	La Perouse, Maddens Plains, Curra Moors (Royal NP).

Family Epacridaceae

Description

Erect shrub, to 1 m tall, with distinctive concave, sharp-tipped, spreading leaves which are stem-clasping, to 2 cm long. Flowers pink, with 5 spreading narrow triangular lobes. Up to 20 flowers are borne in conspicuous clusters at the end of branches. Fruit a tiny capsule, about 1.5 mm long.

Flowering period	Aug. to Oct.
Distribution	Widespread in sandstone areas of the Sydney district. Occurs all along coast and tablelands of NSW; also Vic, SA and Tas.
Habitat	Wet heath and sedgeland, in full sun.
Notes	The pink flowers of this species can dominate wet heath in spring. The name 'incarnata' is a reference to the flesh-coloured flowers ('carnis' is Latin for 'flesh').
Similar species	None in the region.
Specific sites	Lane Cove NP, Maddens Plains, Curra Moors (Royal NP).

Family Stylidiaceae

Description

Perennial plant, with grass-like leaves rising from the base of flowering stem. Leaves linear, as short as 8 cm or as long as 25 cm. A single flowering stem, to 40 cm tall, bears pink flowers along the upper part. Flowers have 4 spreading petals and a column which is bent like a trigger below the flower when 'set'. It is released when an insect lands on the flower, moving quickly to hit the visitor on the back, thus depositing or picking up pollen.

Flowering period	Sept. to Dec.
Distribution	Widespread throughout the Sydney district and in many other areas of the State; also Qld, Vic, Sa and Tas.
Habitat	Open forest, in sandy soil.
Notes	The sensitive column works best on sunny days. It resets a short time after 'firing'.
Similar species	*S. productum* has tufts of leaves on stems above the ground, not rising from the base. *S. lineare* is a much smaller plant, with leaves 2–4 cm long.
Specific sites	Pennant Hills Park, Oatley Park, Windsor Downs NR.

251

Family Stylidiaceae

Description

Soft branched undershrub, to 1.5 m tall, with narrow spreading leaves crowded along the stems, to 40 mm x 1 mm. Pale pink flowers are arranged on branching stems to 4 cm long, well above the leafy stems. White flowered forms are sometimes found. Like all *Stylidium*, this plant has a sensitive column which is triggered by insects.

Flowering period	Aug. to Nov.
Distribution	Scattered throughout the Sydney district and in many other areas of the State; also Qld and Vic.
Habitat	Open forest, usually on protected or rocky sites.
Notes	The name is a reference to the larch-like leaves. The larch is a European conifer with narrow leaves.
Similar species	None in the region.
Specific sites	The Basin (Campbelltown), Bents Basin (Nepean River), Winifred Falls (Royal NP).

Family Epacridaceae

Description

Rigid spreading shrub, to 1.5 m tall. Leaves ovate to lance-shaped, tapering to a fine sharp tip, slightly concave above, to 20 mm x 10 mm. Flowers tubular, erect or spreading, to 20 mm long, bearded inside, with 5 lobes rolled back exposing the stamens, mostly lime green but turning pink with age. Fruit 5-angled, succulent, about 7 mm long.

Flowering period	March to July.
Distribution	Restricted to Sydney and Blue Mountains. Occurs to the north, west and south in a variety of poor soils.
Habitat	Open forest, woodland and heath, in sandstone soils, sandy clay and alluvium.
Notes	Petals roll back to reveal hairs in throat. The fruit is edible.
Similar species	*S. angustifolia* has pendulous flowers and leaves with minutely toothed margins.
Specific sites	Castlereagh NR, Windsor Downs NR, Oatley Park.

Family Epacridaceae

Description

Low spreading shrub, to 1 m tall. Leaves oblong-linear, sharp-tipped, convex above, to 15 mm x 3 mm. Flowers red, tubular, to 25 mm long, with 5 bearded lobes which are rolled back and 5 pink stamens extending beyond the tube. Flowers spreading or drooping, borne singly in leaf axils. Fruit rounded, succulent, about 5 mm long.

Flowering period	April to Aug.
Distribution	Widespread in sandstone areas of the Sydney district, extending to Blue Mountains. Occurs all along coast and tableland of NSW.
Habitat	Woodland and heath, in sandy soil.
Notes	Abundant red tubular flowers make this species conspicuous and easy to identify, especially as it flowers in autumn and winter.
Similar species	None in the region.
Specific sites	Woronora Dam Road, Devlins Creek (North Epping), Scheyville NP.

Family Myrtaceae

Description

Erect tree, to 40 m tall, with dense dark foliage. Bark fibrous and persistent. Leaves opposite and at ends of branches in whorls of 4, elliptic, dark dull green above, pale underneath, to 10 cm x 4 cm. Buds and flowers in globular clusters on long stalks. Flowers cream, with numerous free stamens, followed by a woody capsule consisting of a number of united fruit, about 15 mm diameter.

Flowering period	Oct. to Dec.
Distribution	Widespread in the Sydney district. A major component of the forests which originally grew on Wianamatta Shale soils of the inner western suburbs. Extending all along coast and lower tablelands of NSW; also Qld.
Habitat	Eucalypt forest, often on slopes and in gullies, usually on shale or shale-sandstone interface.
Notes	An important timber tree because of its resistance to termites and marine borers. The name 'syn-carpia' means 'united fruit'.
Similar species	None in the region.
Specific sites	Poulton Park (Oatley Bay), Ashfield Park, Yaralla (Concord West).

Family Proteaceae

Description

Erect slender shrub, to 3 m tall, often multi-stemmed from the base but with few branches. Leaves large, leathery, obovate, irregularly toothed, with prominent veins above, to 18 cm x 5 cm. Flowers red, in dense compact heads, to 15 cm across, surrounded by bright red bracts, to 9 cm long. There may be up to 250 individual flowers; lower flowers open first. Fruit a woody canoe-shaped follicle, to 15 cm long.

Flowering period	Sept. to Oct.
Distribution	Widespread in the Sydney district, extending north to Watagan Mts, south to Southern Highlands and west to Blue Mountains.
Habitat	Open forest, in sandy soil.
Notes	The floral emblem of NSW. The botanical name means 'most beautiful species seen from afar'.
Similar species	None in the region.
Specific sites	Warrah Sanct. (Patonga), Sphinx–Bobbin Head, Engadine–Kangaroo Creek.

Family Tremandraceae

Description

Low spreading shrub, to 30 cm tall, with leaves mostly opposite, linear, rough with small glandular hairs, margins curled under, to 20 mm x 2 mm. Flowers 4-petalled, pink with dark centre, hanging like a bell, borne singly from leaf axils. Flower stalks have dark red glandular hairs.

Flowering period July to Jan.

Distribution Restricted to sandstone areas north and north-west of Sydney.

Habitat Heath and scrub, in sandy soil.

Notes The small dark red glandular hairs on the flower stem and sepals help separate this species from other *Tetratheca*.

Similar species *T. ericifolia* and *T. neglecta* do not have glandular hairs and each have leaves in whorls.

Specific sites Manly Reservoir, Maroota, Salvation Track (Ku-ring-gai Chase).

Family Tremandraceae

Description

Erect undershrub, to 60 cm tall, with stems shortly hairy. Leaves in whorls of 4–5, each leaf elliptic, with margins curled under, to 20 mm x 8 mm. Flowers 4-petalled, pink with dark centre, hanging like a bell, borne singly from leaf axils. Flower stalks and sepals have soft white hairs.

Flowering period	Aug. to Nov.
Distribution	Scattered in the Sydney district, extending to Blue Mountains and Southern Highlands. Occurs all along NSW coast and tablelands; also Qld and Vic.
Habitat	Open forest, woodland and heath, in sandy soil.
Notes	The only *Tetratheca* in the Sydney district with elliptic leaves in whorls.
Similar species	None in the region.
Specific sites	Oxford Falls, Picton Lakes (Thirlmere), Curra Moors (Royal NP).

Family Orchidaceae

Description

Ground orchid, to 50 cm tall, with a solitary narrow leaf, to 20 cm long. Flower spike with up to 10 pale blue flowers marked with darker blue dots on upper petals and sepals. Flowers about 3 cm wide, the column with rows of yellow calli and tufts of white hairs. Flowers usually open on warmer days.

Flowering period	Aug. to Oct.
Distribution	Widespread in the Sydney district and along most of the NSW coast and tablelands; also Qld, Vic, SA, Tas and NZ.
Habitat	Open forest and heath, in damp sandy soil.
Notes	The spotted sepals and petals separate this species from other local *Thelymitra*.
Similar species	*T. pauciflora* has smaller flowers without the spots.
Specific sites	Castlereagh NR, Warrah Sanct. (Patonga), Curra Moors Track (Royal NP).

259

Family Anthericaceae

Description

Erect herb, to 60 cm tall, with cylindrical tubers on the roots,
1–3 cm long. A few leaves near stem base, linear, 20–50 cm long.
Flower stems much-branched, bearing up to 8 purple flowers.
These have 6 petal-like segments (tepals); the outer 3 tepals narrow,
but inner 3 broad with fringed margins. Fruit a small capsule, to
7 mm long, enclosed by the old flower.

Flowering period	Oct. to Dec.
Distribution	Widespread in the Sydney district and throughout much of the State; also Qld, Vic and SA.
Habitat	Open forest, woodland and heath, in sandy soil.
Notes	Tuber edible.
Similar species	*T. juncifolius* is leafless and has ridged flowering stems.
Specific sites	Castlereagh NR, Windsor Downs NR, Oatley Park.

Family Myrtaceae

Description

Small tree, mostly 3–5 m tall in open situations but old trees in sheltered sites may be 25 m tall. Bark light grey, shedding in thin strips. Leaves alternate or crowded near the end of branches, narrow elliptic to lance-shaped, to 12 cm x 3 cm, upper surface dark green, lower surface grey, with scattered oil glands. Flowers yellow, with 5 rounded petals and numerous stamens, borne in clusters near the ends of branches. Fruit a domed 3-valved capsule, to 6 mm diameter.

Flowering period	Dec. to Feb.
Distribution	Scattered north and south of Sydney. Occurs all along coast of NSW; also central tablelands, Qld and Vic.
Habitat	Rocky watercourses, stream banks and rainforest.
Notes	A long-lived tree, common in and around sheltered creeks.
Similar species	*T. collina* occurs away from streams on forested slopes; its leaves have numerous dense oil glands. *Tristania neriifolia* has opposite leaves.
Specific sites	Woronora River, Nortons Basin, Devlins Creek (North Epping).

Family Fabaceae

Description

Erect shrub, mostly 2–3 m tall, with green, striate, terete branches which are apparently leafless and often pendulous. Flowers yellow with red markings, borne in racemes along the ends of wiry stems. Fruit an ovate pod, to 5 mm long.

Flowering period	Oct. to Nov.
Distribution	Widespread in coastal areas of the Sydney district. Occurs all along coast of NSW; also Qld, Vic, SA and WA.
Habitat	Swampy sites in woodland and sandy heath.
Notes	The leafless twiggy nature of this shrub is reflected in the botanical name; 'viminalis' is Latin for 'osier' or 'willow twig', 'juncus' means 'reed-like'.
Similar species	None in the region.
Specific sites	Kurnell, Curra Moors (Royal NP), Maddens Plains.

Family Lamiaceae

Description

Shrub, to 1.5 m tall, often dwarfed in exposed coastal situations, with branches, leaf undersurfaces and calyx covered with dense silky hairs. Leaves in whorls of 4, narrow lance-shaped, usually crowded along the stems, to 25 mm long. Flowers white with mauve or orange spots, to 14 mm long, distinctly 2 lipped, with the lower lip divided into 3 spreading lobes and the upper lip with 2 erect lobes.

Flowering period	Some flowers all year round.
Distribution	Ocean coastline north and south of Sydney and harbour foreshores. Occurs all along NSW coast; also Lord Howe Is.
Habitat	Sandstone cliffs and coastal shrubland.
Notes	Tolerant to salt spray. Commonly cultivated and used for foreshore regeneration.
Similar species	None in the region.
Specific sites	Palm Beach, La Perouse, Kurnell, Curracurrong (Royal NP).

263

Family Epacridaceae

Description

Erect shrub, to 2 m tall, with crowded sharp-tipped leaves, to
12 mm long, ovate, with a rounded base and very small leaf stalk
(1 mm long). Flowers with thin floral tube, 10–12 mm long,
5 spreading broad overlapping lobes, mostly white but sometimes
pink. Flowers borne singly but crowded at the ends of branches in
showy inflorescences.

Flowering period	May to Sept.
Distribution	Common in sandstone areas along coast, extending to Blue Mountains. Occurs all along coast and tablelands of NSW; also Qld.
Habitat	Open forest, heath and coastal dunes.
Notes	*Woollsia* is a monotypic genus, the one species being restricted to NSW and Qld.
Similar species	None in the region.
Specific sites	La Perouse, West Head, Kurnell, Waterfall (Heathcote NP).

Family Xanthorrhoeaceae

Description

Perennial plant with thick underground stem and long crowded tough leaves rising from the base of the plant at ground level. Trunk usually absent, but if present, only to 50 cm tall. Leaves glossy green, diamond shaped in cross section and about 2.5 mm wide. Flower stem to 1.5 m long, topped by a smaller flower spike, 30–80 cm long. Flowers numerous but small, followed by woody pointed seed capsules.

Flowering period	Chiefly Aug. to March, depending on fire frequency.
Distribution	Widespread and common in the Sydney district. Occurs north to Goulburn Valley and west to Blue Mountains.
Habitat	Exposed sandstone ridges and hillsides.
Notes	A useful plant for Aboriginal people. It was a source for resin, the base of the leaves were eaten, flowers contain nectar to make a sweet drink and flower spikes were used to make spears.
Similar species	*X. resinifera* occurs on damper sites; it has flat-triangular leaves. *X. arborea* has a trunk and leaves 5–7 mm wide.
Specific sites	Oatley Park, Windsor Downs NR, Scheyville NP, Curra Moors (Royal NP).

265

Family Proteaceae

Description

Erect shrub or small tree, to 8 m tall. Leaves leathery, elliptic, entire, to 20 cm x 4 cm, with conspicuous yellow veins. Juvenile leaves coarsely toothed and new growth tan with rust-coloured hairs. Flowers small, borne in spikes about 5 cm long. Fruit a woody pear-like follicle, to 9 cm long, which splits into 2 to release 2 winged seeds.

Flowering period	Oct. to Nov.
Distribution	Widespread on sandstone areas of the Sydney district, extending to Blue Mountains and Southern Highlands; also north coast of NSW and Qld.
Habitat	Open forest, woodland and heath, in sandy soil.
Notes	The generic name is descriptive of the fruit, being derived from the Greek 'xylon' (wood) and 'melon' (apple).
Similar species	None in the region.
Specific sites	Kurnell, La Perouse, Bents Basin (Nepean River), Warrah Sanct. (Patonga).

Family Xyridaceae

Description

Perennial plant with erect delicate flower stems, to 40 cm tall.
Leaves in tufts from base of plant, flat to almost terete, to 20 cm long
but only 1 mm wide. Leaves with transverse ridges (more easily
seen when dry). Flowers yellow, with 3 broad petal-like segments,
on a globose flower head, 5–7 mm diameter. This flower head
consists of a series of brownish bracts from which the flowers
appear in succession on sunny days.

Flowering period	Nov. to Dec.
Distribution	Widespread along coastal zone of Sydney district, extending to Blue Mountains. Occurs all along NSW coast; also Qld and Vic.
Habitat	Damp sandy heath and edges of swamps.
Notes	Individual flowers short-lived, but replaced by new flowers from the compact round flower head.
Similar species	There are 4 other *Xyris* in the district. They differ only in small ways in the nature of the leaves and shape of flower head and bracts.
Specific sites	Curra Moors (Royal NP), Walumarra Track (Royal NP), Kariong.

Family Rutaceae

Description

Erect to spreading shrub, to 1 m tall, with hairless branches,
prominently ridged. Leaves divided into 3 leaflets, linear, to 4 cm
long, with an acute apex and margins curled underneath. Flowers
white to pink, with 4 petals and 4 stamens, borne in small clusters
from leaf axils on stalks about as long as the leaves. Fruit a small
warty capsule.

Flowering period	July to Oct.
Distribution	Widespread on sandstone areas of the Sydney district. Occurs along most of NSW coast and tablelands; also Qld.
Habitat	Open forest, woodland and heath, in sandy soil.
Notes	Distinguished from other *Zieria* in the area by its hairless branches, narrow leaflets and flowers on stalks about as long as leaflets.
Similar species	*Z. smithii* is larger and its elliptic leaflets are dotted with oil glands. *Z. pilosa* is smaller and has hairy branches.
Specific sites	Lucas Heights, West Head, O'Hares Creek (Darkes Forest).

GLOSSARY

acuminate — Tapering to a point.

acute — Pointed, having a sharp tip.

alternate — Arranged at different levels along a stem.

anther — Part of stamen which bears pollen.

apex — The tip (of a leaf).

aril — Fleshy appendage surrounding the surface of a seed, often brightly coloured.

aristate — Bearing a needle-like bristle.

axil — The angle between the stem and the leaf.

axillary — Arising from the axil.

bipinnate — A compound leaf which is twice divided, into pinnae, thence into pinnules.

bracteole — A bract-like structure on the flower stalk or calyx.

calyx — All the sepals of a flower.

capsule — A dry fruit which splits to release its seeds.

carpel — Female part of flower which encloses the ovules.

ciliate — Fringed with hairs.

cordate — Heart-shaped (as in leaf base).

decumbent — Stems growing along ground but with tips growing upwards.

dioecious — Male and female flowers on different plants.

dissected — Divided into segments.

drupe — Succulent fruit enclosing a single seed.

elliptic — Oval shaped, broadest at middle.

endemic — Only found within a defined area.

entire — Leaf margins without teeth.

epiphytic — Plant living on another plant but not parasitic.

exserted — Projecting beyond.

falcate — Sickle-shaped.

filament — The stalk of a stamen.

follicle — Dried fruit opening along one line.

funicle — Stalk of ovule or seed

genus — (pl. genera) A group of closely related species.

glabrous	Without hairs.	*obovate*	Ovate but widest above middle.
glaucous	Blue-green in colour with a whitish powdery coating.	*obtuse*	Blunt or rounded at apex.
globose	Spherical, ball-shaped.	*ovate*	Egg-shaped in flat section.
habit	The general appearance of a plant.	*panicle*	A much-branched inflorescence.
		pendulous	Hanging down.
heath	Low plant community dominated by close growing shrubs.	*peduncle*	The stalk of a flower.
		perennial	Living for more than one growing season.
hispid	Densely covered with short stiff hairs.	*phyllode*	Modified leaf stalk acting like a leaf (as in some wattles).
inflorescence	The flowering arrangement of a plant.	*pinna/ae*	The first segment of a compound or divided leaf.
interjugary	Glands present on leaf stalks of wattles between pairs of pinnae.	*pinnate*	A compound leaf divided once into leaflets.
		pinnule	The ultimate leaflet of a divided (bipinnate) leaf.
juvenile	Young stage of growth.	*pod*	The dried fruit (of a pea).
kino	Reddish sap from bark of trees.		
lanceolate	Lance-shaped, broadest below middle and tapering to a pointed apex.	*prostrate*	Lying flat on the ground.
		pubescent	Covered with short soft hairs.
leaflet	A segment of a compound leaf.	*raceme*	Unbranched inflorescence of stalked flowers.
lignotuber	Woody swelling at the base of some plants containing dormant buds.	*revolute*	Rolled under (as leaf margins).
		rhachis	The axis of a compound leaf.
linear	Long, narrow, with parallel sides.	*rosette*	Radiating cluster of leaves at the base of a stem.
monoecious	Male and female flowers separate but on the same plant.	*scape*	Upright flowering stem.
mucro	Sudden sharp point.	*sepal*	One of the segments, usually green, backing a flower.
obcordate	Heart-shaped and notched at apex.		
oblong	Rectangular, longer than wide.	*sessile*	Without a stalk.

spike	Unbranched inflorescence of stalkless flowers.	twiner	A climbing plant which supports itself with twisting stems.
stamen	Male organ of flower, consisting of anther and filament.	umbel	A flower structure in which all the flower stalks rise from one point, umbrella-like.
stipule	Pair of appendages at the base of a leaf.	umbellate	In the form of an umbel.
striate	Striped with longitudinal ridges.	undulate	Wavy (as in leaf margins).
style	Part of flower above ovary which bears the stigma.	valve	Segment of a woody fruit.
subspecies	A grouping within species used to indicate geographical variants.	villous	Covered with long weak hairs.
		whorl	A ring of leaves from the same level of the stem.
succulent	Fleshy or juicy.	woodland	Plant community dominated by short trees spaced so that there is grass or shrubs between them.
terete	Cylindrical.		
terminal	At the end or apex.		
tomentose	Covered with matted short hairs.		
tomentum	Woolly short matted hairs.		

REFERENCES AND FURTHER READING

Benson, D. and Howell, J. (1995). *Taken for Granted. The bushland of Sydney and its suburbs*, Royal Botanic Gardens, Sydney.

Benson, D., Ondinea, D. and Bear, V. (1999). *Missing Jigsaw Pieces. The bushland of the Cooks River Valley*, Royal Botanic Gardens, Sydney.

Costermans, L. (1985). *Native Trees and Shrubs of South-eastern Australia*, Rigby, Adelaide.

Ecology of Sydney plant species, Parts 1–7a. Cunninghamia, Vols. 3(2)–6(2), (1993–1999), National Herbarium of New South Wales.

Fairley, A. and Moore, P. (2000 revised). *Native Plants of the Sydney District*, Kangaroo Press, Sydney.

Harden, G.J. (1990–1993). *Flora of New South Wales*, Vols. 1–4, New South Wales University Press, Kensington.

Howell, J. and Benson, D. (2000). *Sydney's Bushland. More Than Meets the Eye*, Royal Botanic Gardens, Sydney.

Howell, J., McDougall, L. and Benson, D. (1995). *Riverside Plants of the Hawkesbury–Nepean*, Royal Botanic Gardens, Sydney.

Jones, D. and B. (2000). *Native Orchids of Southern Australia*, Bloomings Books, Hawthorn, Victoria.

Olde, P. and Marriott, N. (1994–1995). *The Grevillea Book*, Vols. 1–3, Kangaroo Press, Sydney.

Robinson, L. (1994). *Field Guide to the Native Plants of Sydney*, Kangaroo Press, Sydney.

Tame, T. (1992). *Acacias of Southeast Australia*, Kangaroo Press, Sydney.

INDEX